In Memory of Winfried "Winni" Fries (February 19, 1938 – May 27, 2015)

A true ace of the track!

Winni's passions were motorcycle- and Grand-Tourisme-Class racing (up to 1600 ccm). His greatest victory was in 1968 with his Alfa Romeo when he crossed the finish line before Huschke von Hanstein, a Porsche works driver in a Porsche. As a motorcycle racer, he also received World Champion points: 1974 in 350 ccm class on Yamaha 5 points and Kreidler 6 points. Winni was a private rider and achieved success without any type of sponsoring.

Well known on the track, his career included races in Germany, Belgium and the Netherlands on numerous occasions.

Although my grandfather, Emil, introduced my father to motorcycle racing, he let him know that he was not impressed with the motor sport. In fact, one day he got so upset that he chopped my father's bike in half with an axe, but that did not stop my dad. My father's first racing bike was an Italian Rumi, a loaner from the Regitz company in order to participate in his first motorcycle race in Neunkirchen, West Germany.

Here are some memories from my sister, Diana: I was seven years old when my dad came home one day from victory lane with a laurel made of gold-tone leaves and a trophy. Many people came over to the house to congratulate him and the phone wouldn't stop ringing.

On his way to the AVUS race in East Berlin, he was detained at the border for quite some time because he had to shave off his mustache since he had none on his passport picture. His assistant, Norbert, was asleep in the back of the VW Bus and was spotted by the security guard who said that if he had time to sleep, he could wait to pass until the next day. When dad finally convinced the security guard that he was going to be late for the race, they arranged for an escort to the race track.

When I was 10, I got my own victory lap after the race on the racing bike sitting behind my dad, giving me a taste for speed. It was an unforgettable experience, especially the low leans in the curves.

At the III ADAC race of the Middle Rhein on June 9 [1968], at the Nürburgring, motorist Winfried Fries from Mosberg-Richweiler [Saarland], now residing in Oberkirchen [Saarland], achieved a great victory. He won with his Alfa-Romeo-Spider in the Grand-Tourisme-Class up to 16 ccm with a brilliant time of 59 Minutes and 45 seconds. With the golden laurel his club Motorsportvereinigung "Allerburg" received yet another trophy. Winfried Fries, age 30, has been active in the motorsport for years and in the past year was able to achieve good placements at seven national motorcycle races throughout the Bundesrepublik. The Saarbrücker newspaper congratulates this successful sports motorist's win at Nürburgring. Pictured is Fries with his Tourenwagen and the laurel. Foto: Carl

Acknowledgements

I want to thank

My sister,
Dr. Diana Pengitore, ND, American Translator Association (ATA) member, and freelance translator residing in Virginia Beach, Virginia, USA, for her expert translation from German to English, which was long overdue, and her additional research.

My brother in law,
Dr. Frank Pengitore, Ed. D., for his editorial expertise in bringing this publication forth.

Dr. Carl Fusco, ND, NMD, for his technical advice regarding motorcycle skills. He is also a member of the Sons of Poseidon Veteran's riding group in Virginia Beach, Virginia, USA.

Norbert Blasius and Valentin Scheer, my father's constant companions, especially during the most challenging times of his racing career, for supplying vital information for this book.

My friends, Ralf Hauprich and Ralf Hartmann, for their statements.

STOP **How to Read this Handbook**

Please read this manual carefully as it includes vital information to a safe approach when riding the Nürburgring-Nordschleife at a high speed. **Do not skip sections of this book.** They are meant to be read in the order presented. Study the materials and remember to practice, practice, practice, so that you can ride the Ring safely and enjoy it.

This handbook shows track sections on the left page with photographs corresponding to the boxed areas on the sketch to the right with approximate speeds. Note, due to the variations of rider and bike weights, speed and results may vary while riding this track. This does not take into consideration individual rider technique.

!!! Ride at your own risk!!!

The so called "Green Hell" is 20.8 km long and is located in the Eifel, Germany. Opened in June of 1927, it has claimed over 200 lives.

The photos show bicyclists during a bicycle event on the Nordschleife, which allowed me to take these photographs. Additional information is in the section "The Nürburgring-Nordschleife!"

This book is a translation from the German book, *Ein As auf der Nürburgring-Nordschleife*. Therefore, the terms concerning the Nordschleife are not subject to variation. This means that in some cases there is no direct translation for them from German into English. I did put the translatable terms in English behind the German expression in parentheses. If you go on the track, all the signs are in German, so you need to know the German names.

The drawings are taken from the German version. The speed information is in km/h[1]. When you read "Bild," this means photograph; "Kuppe" means knoll – you cannot see where the road goes behind it; and, "Brücke" means Bridge.

Ambiguous meanings are clarified in footnotes; only the appropriate definition is given. To have a complete understanding of a word, you need to look it up in a good dictionary.

[1] I mile = 1.6 kilometers.

What's with this Speeding?

Some say it's the kick, but no that's not it. Personally, I can refuse any kick. When at 210 km/h your rear wheel starts to slide uncontrollably, there is "kick" to no end. It's a strong sensation in your stomach. It's different when you have control over the bike with your knee firmly on the ground and you know exactly where you are, 100%.

Riding a motorcycle is a piece of freedom. One becomes one with the machine, just one feeling, the road and you. And if you're going really fast, there is no time for thoughts. Thoughts are too slow in this fast-paced world. You ride and know that this is the absolute peak of concentration – there is no other level. Concentration to complete freedom. Anyone who is speed-oriented will second that; others are continuously afraid of being passed by fears and worries!

Wolfgang Fries

This book is dedicated to those who can handle high speed and who have enough sense to do it in areas where they can assess potential danger.

"He who knows danger, can face it!"

An Ace at the
Nürburgring-Nordschleife

- Handbook -

Imprint

Copyrights and clearances

I wish to thank the Nürburgring Automotive GmbH marketing department for approving the German script, the photographs and the drawings.

Book design and typeset:

Wolfgang Fries
Contact: Friesway@online.de

Translator: Dr. Diana M. Pengitore, ND
Editor: Dr. Frank Pengitore, Ed. D.
Technical motorcycle advisor: Dr. Carl Fusco, ND, NMD

Production and publishing:

BoD - Books on Demand GmbH
In de Tarpen 42
22848 Norderstedt; Deutschland

ISBN: 978-3-7528-6921-7

Bibliografische Information der Deutschen Nationalbibliothek
Die Deutsche Nationalbibliothek verzeichnet diese Publikation in der Deutschen Nationalbibliografie; detaillierte bibliografische Daten sind im Internet über http://dnb.d-nb.de abrufbar.
(The book is listed in the German Nationalbibliografie; detailed information is available at: http://dnb.d-nb.de)

Statements from Two Experienced Motorcyclists.

Point of View

For a few years when I was on the road with Wolli I thought, "You must be a little bit crazy to have a trip[1] like that because riding faster would be completely insane." I luckily escaped several rough encounters and situations and decided to put an end to the "high-speed-existence" on public roads – it was time for the checkered flag. I had reached a point where my good luck was used up, and a bad accident was just a matter of time. During that time, high speed was the ultimate experience and best in a low lean!

Today I see it differently, from the view of experience of that time with awareness of experienced danger that this action brought with it. Today, speeding has a different meaning for me. Safety comes first, only then can one enjoy it 100%. I have made it my first rule to arrive back home without being wrecked after each ride.

I also wish to emphasize that less-experienced motorcyclists do not want to be harassed about their riding skills. Very dangerous!!! Just like it is the responsibility of an experienced biker not to bully a "greenhorn" into death. Ride your own ride! Of course, on the race track things look a bit different.

"So, guys, take care of yourselves and stay on your bike. Have fun, but be safe and only then will you enjoy the ride. Safety first!!!"

Ralf Hauprich

Friendships

I met many bikers in pubs. During some conversations I felt uneasy wondering if I could keep up with the first group ride. But afterwards my companions dubbed me completely crazy. Over a period of years, this resulted in me hanging out with two crazy biker friends.

When someone has reached his mental limits, but not those of the bike, and he continues to race recklessly, then the leader must be crazy!? Wolfgang and I met in 1999, although I knew his name and reputation from the time with the moped[2].

We were introduced by an old biker friend not in a pub. During our first ride together, I reached a point where I thought "he must be crazy," but I soon rejected that thought and made an effort to keep up with his speed. That's how we rode quite a lot of curves in the Eifel where between Wolfgang's rear tire and the green stripe no folded-up New York Times could have fit.

Ralf Hartmann

PS: I can remember the two statements from Ralf which continue to bring a grin, "So, in the last right downhill I thought, 'Now he is going to run out of road!' 'When riding the Nordschleife with you there is almost no danger of being passed.'"

---

[1] Trip: (slang) an experience that is pleasing, exciting, unusual, etc.

[2] Moped: a small motorcycle; originally it was a bicycle equipped with a motor.

An Ace at the Nürburgring-Nordschleife

- Handbook -

Contents

The Beginning

Let's start where it all began. My first name is Wolfgang and when I asked my father why this name, he answered, "During my youth it was the first name of the fastest car racer in Germany – Wolfgang Count Berghe von Trips[1]." It wasn't enough that I had this name. My father was a driving instructor and an inspired car and motorcycle racer, although he was more interested in motorcycle racing, and this was his way of passing his enthusiasm for this sport on to me. With pride he told me that he had passed Giacomo Agostini – multiple world champion – with a Yamaha 350 downhill at the Fuchsröhre on the Nürburgring.

Back then I laid down on the racing bike of my farther, barely reaching the bars with my hands and imagined what racing was like.

When I was eight, I sat for the first time as a driver on a MV Agusta, an operational window display model, able to do 50 km/h. To that I must say that my daddy for weeks pulled our leg about getting a small motorcycle. One day a large box arrived. It was the model from the window display and bright red in color. My brother and I knew immediately what this was about. Although he was not in complete agreement, I unpacked the bike, grabbed a gasoline can, and got this thing to run. It was really exciting!

On Sunday, September 25, 1977, when I was 11 the nightmare for any motorcyclist happened to my father, an accident at the Hockenheimring[2]. It took place right after the start in the first curve. The cause was a single rider using newly introduced racing slicks (treadless tires adopted from drag racing) that had not been properly warmed up during two routine preliminary runs that were normally required prior to each race. He lost control right after the start and was separated from his bike that hit the sidewall and then spun back onto the track. It was a massive crash that involved five other riders, who all sustained injuries. My father, who could no longer escape, hit the bike, crashed and broke his spine.

He was immediately airlifted via helicopter to the nearby Ludwigshafen Hospital (a specialty clinic for paralysis and burn victims among other things) where he spent a grueling 12 months mostly lying in bed and taking physical therapy to adjust to his new existence in the wheelchair, the result of having been paralyzed in the crash.

This accident, of course, affected all of us. We were devastated! In fact, my sister, Diana, gave up motorcycling for good. His inspiration for racing never stopped and despite his paralysis, he continued in his profession as a driving instructor and supported my brother Michael's and my motorcycling.

At 15, I rode in a motocross race. During the first run I fell down twice, but still took 26th place – one before my brother. At this race the current stars Harald Ott, Joachim Jasinski, etc. participated. They were the up-and-coming beginners on the scene – an international field with 33 riders.

[1]Wolfgang Alexander Albert Eduard Maximilian Reichsgraf Berghe von Trips (* 4. Mai 1928 in Köln; † 10. September 1961), a German Formula 1 race car driver. At the Italian Grand Prix in 1961, he lost control of his Ferrari and crashed into a stand full of spectators. Sixty people were injured, killing 15 and himself.

[2]Hockenheimring: race track in Germany.

At the second run, I took the lead to the first curve finishing in sixth place. I never really took a liking to motocross, so I stopped. After the moped I had when I was 15, I acquired a Yamaha RD 80 MX when I turned 16. A beater, it couldn't even manage the fifth gear on a flat road. But with my father's help, who had much experience as an auto mechanic, we were able to breathe some new life into that 80's model. After the mounting of a full fairing, it reached a speed of 120 km/h.

At 18, I rode a RD 350, which I wrecked six months later in a curve, due to a new front tire. Once your front tire slides away from you, often times there is not much you can do. Lesson learned, and since then after mounting new tires I took coarse sandpaper and sanded down the smooth, shiny surfaces.

In 1986, at age 20, I acquired a used Kawa GPZ 900 R, probably one of the fastest bikes you could ride at that time, 117 hp, speedometer 270 km/h, except for the brake, which was a catastrophe. If you encountered a bump in a curve you would still "Rock'n Roll" after 200 meters. That was too dangerous for me, so I sold that thing. I mentioned this fault to the buyer, and we met again two weeks later, when he stated that that thing holds the road well. I wonder what had been the cause?!

My dream of course was an FZR 1000 that I fulfilled one year later. An insane bike with 135 hp, a four-piston brake system in front per disk, a deltabox-frame, 229 kg wet weight, and a 160 mm rear tire. Today I can laugh about it, but in any case, this moped hugged the curves superbly. At first the tires were a catastrophe, but later things improved.

In 1990, I took a break and shifted my attention to more important things. In 1995 I started to ride again. Indecisive about what to ride, and after much back and forth, I again bought the old FZR. I valued the advantages, a relatively high profile that actually provided protection from the wind and was not for show, and a relatively low weight. The newer FZRs were heavier and more powerful. I sat in the motorcycle and not on top, and the sitting position was comfortable. In comparison to the 1000 models, the old one resembled a 600 model.

After a frontal crash with a car in 1998, I made arrangements to buy another one; I had no choice. Later on, on occasion I rode a Yamaha R1. I was not impressed by it. I experienced the full force of the wind due to the small cowling, and every time I used the brakes I got the feeling of summersaulting to the front – I was always lifted out of the seat with ease. It was different with my old FZR. When braking, I could really support myself on the bars. The bike's forces were distributed in a way that resulted in a linear pressure and not in a circular one like a torque.

Incidentally, it used to always give me the greatest pleasure when I blew by the R1-boys on the Nordschleife on my old FZR, leaving them in the dust. ☺

Technique

Blinded by the appearance of the bike, many forget the most important aspect, the technical attributes. From a technical point of view, the bike must always be cutting edge, starting with the tire profile and pressure, which should be checked regularly and before each run on the "Ring."

Here is a quote from Ulrich Thomson's own riders manual about the Nürburgring, "On fast bikes the centrifugal force of the tires is increased to the point where the small site valve spring can be compressed. At this rate of speed this can lead to an insidious and fatal loss of tire pressure. To prevent this, it is suggested to substitute metal valve caps with a rubber seal." The same goes for the brake pads, never wait for them to wear out completely; change them early.

The master mechanic of my motorcycle service department told me that according to the owner's manual the brake lines must be changed after four years. Do it! Also install the flexible braided stainless steel brake lines, since they do not have any pressure loss from expansion even after long term use. Remember to change your brake fluid every two years according to the manufacturer's recommendation.

Brake fluid is hygroscopic, meaning moisture absorbent. When you have a certain amount of water in the brake fluid and while riding really fast, always waiting until the last moment to brake, the brake will heat up and the water will start to boil - you will end up with air in your brake system. That means you will no longer have any brake pressure! Be diligent about the safety of your bike, there are plenty of other dangers where you can break your neck. Believe me!

Also check the oil and coolant levels on a regular basis and before every long ride. It is expensive to burn up the engine. Also check the slack of the drive chain - refer to the technical manual. In case you dismounted and mounted the rear wheel, check the chain after riding 5 km to ensure that it still has sufficient slack.

If the chain is too tight after mounting, it will result in additional tension, leading to damage to the gear box – an expensive matter! Grease your chain regularly, especially when the rollers start to turn silver since usually they are black. Don't buy cheap chain spray; invest in something of quality so that your expensive chain will last. Take it down when it is stretched out or pulled out of shape and has too much side slack - again, refer to your technical manual.

A really safety-oriented biker marks the nuts and screws with a small line of paint, in case the vibration causes a loosening of the nut, making it immediately noticeable by the movement of the paint mark. Furthermore, screws are not continuously tightened up during regular check-ups without a torque wrench. The old metal worker knows very well: Don't over tighten! Take care of your machine, it is a part of your life insurance.

Other safety concerns: Always wear safety gear. Always! Often times accidents happen during a short ride to town. "Summer-gear" is available; it has numerous small perforations in the leather, allowing for good or excellent ventilation. Also, there is all-weather gear.

Actual event: In 1999 I crashed near the end of Pflanzgarten at 220 km/h after the second hill. At this location I was thrown off due to the high speed. I went airborne and landed again at a slight angle – then I lost control and tumbled along the road without colliding with any other object! Except for a disc tear in the lumber region, I walked away with minor injuries thanks to the protective gear.

Wheel Suspension

The original configuration from Öhlins was too stiff. The suspension strut was not working correctly, resulting in rear wheel hop in a curve with an uneven surface. So I grabbed the shop manual and followed the guidelines precisely. I reset the spring preload as well as the compression and rebound stages. Until then I had no clue about this area of expertise, so I bought a book and studied it. There wasn't much to it. Compression stage simply means the resistance of the spring as it deflects. The rebound stage is the retardation of the spring during its bounce-back. Compression and rebound stages must have the same settings. Very easy! The specs page also gave precise directions when the stages were either set too high or too low. So I adjusted it and drove, re-adjusted it and drove again, always the same course, and, sure enough, the wheel suspension started to work.

Before it was just too stiff, but after the adjustment, it was superb! It was clear to see on the shoulder of the rear tire. Prior to this, the acceleration line on the tire was located in the inner third of the tire, but now I could definitely see the rubbing on the lower third, and I noticed a huge improvement when accelerating out of the curve. The rear tire definitely had more grip, and the wheel suspension was now able to keep the rear tire on the ground.

Braking

Most motorcycle junkies crave more horsepower. Why? Just to ride straight ahead? I went ahead and installed Spiegler cast iron brake discs, braided stainless steel brake lines, Whitepower fork springs in the front, Öhlins wheel suspension in the rear, and a shorter gear ratio. Previously, the bike could do 290 km/h, but now 270 km/h was possible according to the speedometer, which was sufficient, since I rarely rode that fast.

By the way, as a rule, the biggest shortcoming is braking. During outings with other motorcyclists, I usually had a lead of 300 meters after one curve due to braking skills. As a rule, bikers brake poorly. Today's material is light years ahead when it comes to the capability of each biker. Therefore, it is necessary to practice braking. This is best done in an empty parking lot starting with a low speed and then braking until stopped. You should practice for an entire week from a lower to a high speed to develop a feel for the bike. You have to feel it when the front tire locks in order to release the brake. Braking is vital; it must become second nature, and every minute that you practice braking is not a waste of time.

You can be so perfect at braking that when the tire is in the air on approaching the curve, you will remain seated on the bike without falling off.

What good are 160 horses when you have no reins?

A tip about motorcycling. Knowledge brings awareness. Motorcycling is great fun, but it is life-threatening. Read some books about the subject and familiarize yourself with what to watch for, so that you can face danger when it happens.

Cleanliness

I cleaned my bike after every ride even at 10 P.M. It was never really dirty, only flies and dust. I removed the flies and dust with a soft cloth and some dish detergent with a light touch on the rims, since they are polished on the edges and the rest lacquered.

This is where the good quality chain spray paid for itself. There were no oily smears on the rim, which was only slightly dusty. Afterwards, I used a moist sponge with some polish, quickly going over the lacquered parts including the windshield. I finished with a terrycloth – this removed the water streaks.

This process took 20 minutes. You just have to start and be persistent about this ritual. You will enjoy your bike even better when it's clean. By the way, when washing the bike never spray it down with strong water pressure that will cause damage to the electrical system and take off the lubricant on parts of the bike that need it.

Riding style

One of the most challenging tasks during biking is negotiating curves. As a general statement, a rider has very bad orientation about the lean angle he is in, how fast or low he can still ride, etc. When I talked to an older colleague he told me that he preferred ground contact when taking curves. He placed the foot closest to the inner curve at a slight angle on the foot rest. When he rode at an angle, his shoe sole scratched over the road. This was an orientation aid for him, so that he knew where he was in relation to the road.

Well, I did not use the foot, but the knee. I hung myself next to the motorcycle and pulled it down.

By touching the road with the knee, I knew that I still had some space, which allowed me to go 5 km/h faster. Of course, the contact from the knee pad with the street was really hard; it was not a light abrasion.

While riding a bit faster, I noticed that the bike became a bit spongy due to the grip sliding slightly. Riding even faster, the rear tire started to drift away to the point where I stood at an angle. I managed to get it so far where I drifted almost at an angle through a curve at 180 km/h painting black lines with the rear tire on the asphalt. This is not necessary as it will only result in wear.

As mentioned, you can tell from the rubbing on the sides of the tires the degree of the angle that was achieved. Every biker, no matter what type, must be able to reach the maximum lean. Situations can arise when this is necessary. It is not necessary to mark the tire with a chalk line in order to recognize the lean. By the way, the edge of the tire is not necessarily a mark of identification, since I wore it down. Quote from my father, "You will recognize them from their [tire] faces."

"Hanging on" has its advantages. I lifted my rear completely out of the seat and pressed the knee closest to the curve hard against the fairing.

Consequently, I hugged the bike, which allowed for additional support. If you were to bend the knee towards the curve, some stability would be lost. "Hang on" also means a redistribution of weight. The center of gravity of a motorcycle with the rider hanging on lies lower. In comparison to a conventional riding style, it will affect the speed by approximately 5 km/h. Furthermore, a rider can brake later. Usually, speed is reduced by braking on the straight. Hanging on, you can prevent the bike from its tendency to assume a perpendicular position by braking into a lower lean. It is also possible to brake into a more forceful lean without the bike returning to a perpendicular position.

You have the best brake efficiency with front and rear brakes. You can lose control if a tire locks while braking. Therefore, when a tire locks, briefly release the brake and then tap the brake.

Always choose your speed to allow enough room for braking, keeping in mind that you need to make way for oncoming traffic travelling fast. Passing cars in front of you: I constantly had to be on the lookout for an approaching motorcyclist passing a car in a large arc, often not quite under control. No! Orient yourself on the center line when passing and remain there.

You must be aware of the reaction of oncoming traffic. During my active time in Germany, I noticed that the oncoming traffic sees you and moves over to the right edge of the road making room for you. Therefore, riding close to the midline eliminates the need for a large arc when passing. You can comfortably ride between the cars with sufficient space on each side. This is known as lane splitting. Please note: This maneuver might be illegal in some localities. When passing a convoy, only ride a bit faster than the traffic ahead of you. This way when encountering oncoming traffic, you just tap the brake to merge into the lane. You will have better reaction should a driver change lanes.

But there are still stupid riders who attempt to look to the left past the driver in front of them in a long curve to the right. No! You steer where you stare!!! Keep some distance and look to the right. I might add, it is possible prior to passing while on a long stretch approaching the summit to look under the vehicle in front of you for oncoming traffic.

Also, if you are unfamiliar with a road use caution. Never speed into the curve, which will result in taking the lowest lean. Never!!! You ride the road as follows: Look at the layout of the road for the next mile and prepare your line. Then concentrate on the road surface to see if it's clean or if it varies. To concentrate only on the first curve will surely not produce a harmonious line, since the subsequent curve will indicate how you rode into and exited the first curve.

I also constantly observed the biker that looked with the mind instead of the eyes: The "riding" line and action of a person are good indicators of how he thinks and there are a few morons – unbelievable! Thinking is always related information. Accident free straight out thinking is achieved when riding after a professional. You can observe his technique and can learn from it. It is also beneficial when discussing the different aspects of motorcycle riding in detail.

Another tip when following: Sometimes it is just impossible because the riders are too fast. It's best to abstain from this or you will break your neck. Then there are some who constantly make riding errors that lead not only themselves, but also following riders into danger. Develop your own strategy and perfect your skills; only then will you be safe, safe for yourself.

A few times I encountered a situation where I used the brake sooner than the adjacent rider with the result that I made it through the curve, but the other rider did not!

I never took any professional riding classes on the Nordschleife, but it is my opinion that it is an absolute necessity for the sport-oriented rider. These riders understand their job and take the time to learn. I can assure you that there is a lot to learn regarding motorcycling. Another quote from my father, "Once you get your driver's license, the real time for learning starts."

How skilled can you ride? Well, I always maintained the same speed, always with the knee to the ground, always the same style, and I usually was able to remain seated on the bike, unless I crashed into a car. In 1998, I borrowed my father's driving school bike, a 350 RD. What a condition - a street bike, not suitable for racing! Oh, well a bike is better than no bike at all. I generally entered curves with too much force.

Mind you, I was only "a little too fast," not "much too fast!" In any case, one time while going downhill in a curve, the rear tire and then the front tire broke away. The stand came down, and I *almost* hit the ground, thanks to the knee aiding as a bit of support. I grabbed the front brake somewhat, pushed myself off the ground with my knee, and continued to ride, no crash! This only worked because I was not riding "too fast."

Types of Motorcyclists

This book contains words of an "extremist." No one should consider himself to be in any of the four groups of riders. This is my personal opinion.

A word to the racers: The definition of racing is as follows: To ride as fast as possible. This is a skill! Keep in mind open traffic is not the ideal place to do this. The average driver cannot estimate high speed, much less apply it.

Therefore, practice common sense.

Bikers can be categorized roughly into four classes. To start with, the definition of motorcycling in my case is as follows: Riding of a motorbike over the road.

Class 4: The nice weather Sunday afternoon café riders. These guys clean their Harleys on Saturdays in order to ride 10 km on Sundays to the next city café to pose with their bike. Riding with these things is terrible, a lean almost impossible, and a suspension so stiff that you can feel every unevenness in the back. When braking, you should have an anchor that must be deployed early enough to achieve the desired result! I once rode such a thing (around 1990, a Fat Boy 1,348 cc, with a single brake disc in the front and rear), so I know.

Class 3: Here we have the tour-rider. His attention is completely dedicated to the scenery around him. He enjoys the landscape and the airstream.

Class 2: The so called "Street light racers." These boys are really fast in the straight, their concentration resulting in a complete focus on the road and the bike. Braking doesn't really work, nor does riding a calm and elegant line, but when you listen to them – they are definitely the fastest. Riding like that will not qualify you for the pole position.

Class 1: The first-class riders are considered the most skilled of all bikers. They have complete concentration while riding, being one with the motorcycle. They understand their limits and know exactly where to brake when charging into a curve doing 270 km/h that has a speed limit of only 80 km/h. They ride a curve in an elegant line, with maximum lean, and no adjustment, everything falling right into place.

Speed is a mental capability. The rider must have the ability to understand the ride and to convert such into fractions of seconds. There is no time to think if right or wrong – you just know.

An experienced rider only has to look at the course of the road to know what is possible. These guys are in a minority. Out of 1,000 sport motorcyclists, there is only one shining star glowing in the motorcycle sky. "The street light racer" after one ride with such an expert would declare him completely crazy, but only because he is unable to compute such "madness" in his head.

A true ace would never ride like a "bat out of hell" in regular traffic. He knows that falling off is painful, and he is able to control his right hand even if the "street light racer" flies by on the straight. He will only be behind in the next curve.

Speed and safety go hand in hand.

The Nürburgring-Nordschleife

Now I wish to address the Nürburgring-Nordschleife. Although the sketch on this page is outdated, it is a valuable reference because the distance is recorded in km's, which was omitted on the new sketch.

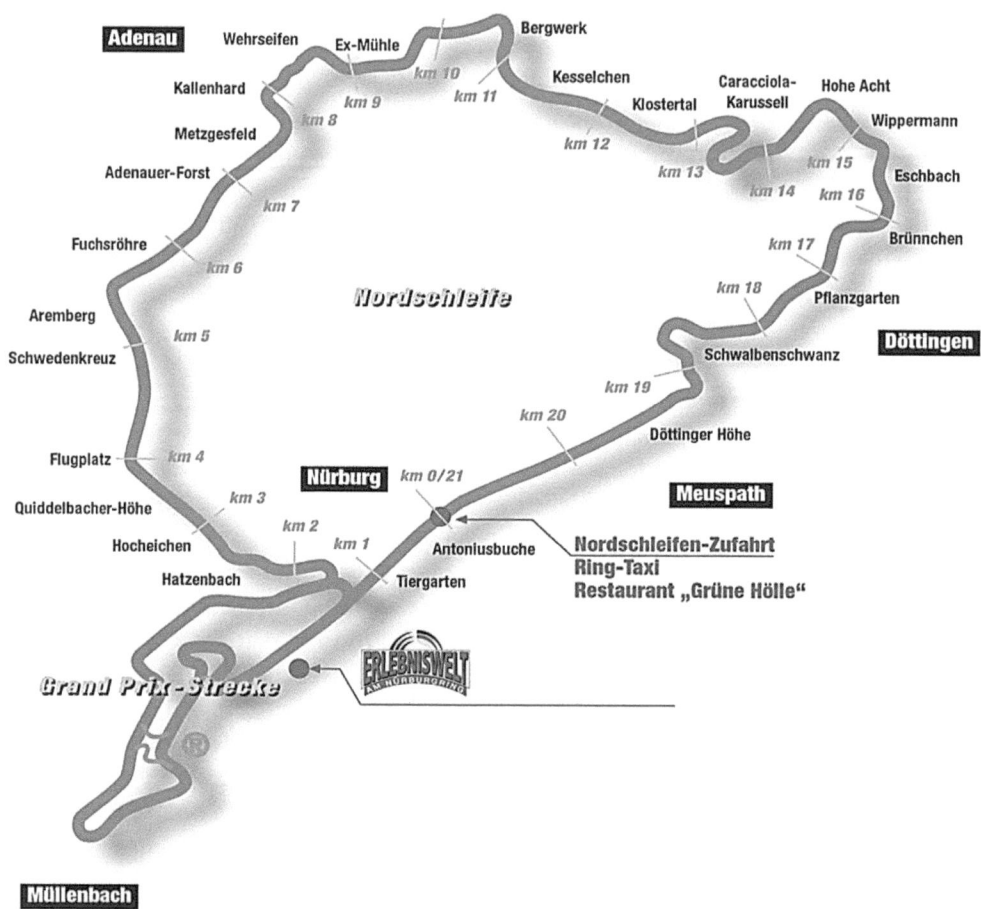

I met "The Green Hell" as a motorcyclist at age 18 on my RD 350. My dad, a highly experienced racer of the Ring, drove ahead in his Ford. Well as an 18-year-old, I was used to riding fast and while following my dad with his squealing tires, I still had sufficient room for a lean.

Therefore, I passed him with no problem. The road was wide with hardly any traffic and had a moderate overview, at least to the Schwedenkreuz. Then the inevitable happened! On the approach to Adenauer Forst, the road suddenly disappeared, and I finished with a bumpy ride into the field. This was a valuable lesson for me. I slowed down a bit because I had no choice since the road had become obscured most of the time.

Another time, while riding through the Karussel, a wild honking Opel Kadett suddenly appeared in my rearview mirror, and, then I didn't understand anything anymore because I thought I was fast.

Three years later I returned to the Ring, this time with the FZR. I concluded that the bike was too fast for the Ring. When turning the throttle just a bit, the bike shot to the front with the next narrow curve in sight. It was time for a motorcycle break. Every once in a while, I felt uncomfortable and the joy of riding had lessened. During that time, I learned a few things about the mind and mental processes. To make it brief, I was able to stop this uncomfortable sensation. The process is simple, just create the same feeling with your thoughts, and it will resolve.

Since riding in my region was not as much fun anymore, I again returned to the Ring. I got acquainted with some annual ticket holders that lived in the region near the track and rode with them on a regular basis. I was able to follow with no problem and when using the brake and in the curve, I always was a bit faster, but somehow when riding alone a bit helpless. During the first few rounds, I experienced definite orientation losses.

This could not continue. I purchased *The Nürburgring Driver Handbook* by Ulrich Thomson. Sad to say, I didn't get much use out of it. There were out of focus and inaccurate images of the track, etc. Also missing was a really good orientation, such as the maximum speed, at each spot. Inadequate manual! I read it twice, then it fell apart, and now it is just a loose collection of pages. Therefore, I wrote my own. ☺ During a bicycle event, I rode the Nordschleife with my bicycle and photographed every section of the track, providing original images and not out-of-focus ones.

Then I bought the video by Helmut Dähne[1], *7:49,71, Der Ring*. Luckily, the camera was set at an angle so that the speedometer was visible. I watched the video and recorded the lowest speeds in the sections corresponding to my sketches. Now I had an orientation.

First, I memorized the sections of the track; they are as follows:
01 Start (Start) at Döttinger Höhe (Döttinger Height)
02 Antoniusbuche (Antonius Beech)
03 Tiergarten (Animal Garden)
04 Hohenrain
05 Alte Boxengasse (Old Pit Row)
06 Hatzenbach (Hatzen Creek)
07 Hocheichen (High Oaks)
08 Quittelbacher Höhe (Quittelbacher Height)
09 Flugplatz (Airport)
10 Schwedenkreuz (Swedish Cross)
11 Arembergkurve (Aremberg Curve)
12 Fuchsröhre (Fox Pipe)
13 Adenauer Forst (Adenauer Forest)
14 Metzgesfeld (Metzges Field)

[1]Dähne, Helmut: Record holder of the Nürburgring-Nordschleife for motorcycles. He also started 23 times at the Isle of Man TT and won it once in 1976. He also won the German "Seriensport" a couple of times (Wikipedia).

15 Kallenhard
16 Wehrseifen
17 Breidscheid
18 Exmühle (Ex Mill)
19 Niki Lauda Links (Niki Lauda Left)
20 Bergwerk (Mine)
21 Kesselchen (Small Kettle)
22 Klostertal (Cloister valley)
23 Karussel (Carousel)
24 Hohe Acht (High Eight)
25 Hedwigshöhe (Hedwigs Height)
26 Wippermann (Wipper Man)
27 Eschbachkuppe (Esch Creek Knoll)
28 Brünnchen (Small Fountain)
29 Eiskurve (Ice Curve)
30 Pflanzgarten (Plant Garden)
31 Schwalbenschwanz (Swallow Tail)
32 Galgenkopf (Gallows Head)
33 Ziel (Finish) at Döttinger Höhe (Döttinger Height)

If you want to become a pro, then you must know the names and include them in your evening prayers. ☺ For example, I always wrote them down, first in numerical order and then adding the names. The next step was the layout of the track and the speeds. You can create a mental image sketch that includes the speeds. The main factor regarding speeds is that you must know the spots with an obstructed view; after all you still have eyes.

Memorize the photographs that I took exactly and also the speeds. This is called visualization. You have to be able to recall the pictures in your memory and be able to ride the entire thing as a movie in your head. If someone wakes you in the middle of the night and says, "Hohe Acht." Then you must know that section of the track and the speed. I can do it.

Might I mention that you can reach really insane speeds and that you will encounter a few "scary curves." I went as fast as 270km/h at times. Of course, the first few laps you will want to ride with a 20 % reduction in speed, thereafter increasing your speed incrementally.

At this high speed, you cannot leave room for errors, NONE! The nine-meter-wide asphalt shrinks to a few centimeters. Everything must match, the breaking point, the angle while entering the curve, the lean, everything!!!

And remember that there is almost no run-off area[1]. Furthermore, you never know the current track conditions. Someone may be standing across the road, or there may be oil or anti-freeze and the like on the track. Be aware of this: **A fast lap on the Nordschleife means one foot in the grave and the other one in the hospital!**

[1] Run-off area: Areas beside the racing track where riders can go if they unintentionally leave the road.

Is there danger in racing? Racing is "negligent suicide!"[1] Over time there is probably no one who has not ended up with broken bones on the track, especially while motorcycle racing.

With my instruction, I will do all I can to assure your safety. However, you will only be as good as your understanding; accidents often happen in a mind fog. It makes no sense to mark each section of the track with a scale to show the degree of difficulty. Difficulty and danger arise with increasing speed. The higher the speed, the higher the risk! Mind you, taking Quiddelbacher Höhe and Exit Pflanzgarten at a high speed will result in a risk that you can no longer assess.

You can become airborne and crash somewhere along the track. Know this: Safety is not guaranteed; you can only approach it.

This is theory, but in reality, there are forces for which you have to make allowances. You have to be physically fit, especially in the areas of muscle mass and endurance. For example, 100 push-ups and a bicycle ride at an average speed of 30 km/h on the speed bike in Saarland going up and down hills had become second nature for me. Nevertheless, the first few laps on the Nürburgring-Nordschleife at the beginning of the season always caused sore muscles!

To be sure, there is danger ahead of you, which is big enough, BUT you can turn it down with your right hand. Also, a great danger lies behind you! As a rookie, you won't master the track, but there are some riders who are really fast. Therefore, don't ride all over the road because you could cause an accident by being mowed down from behind. So, keep an eye on your rearview mirror!

Furthermore, the Nordschleife has more than 25 different surface layers, and the track is continually being upgraded. I never rode in wet conditions, except once when the track was not completely dry. The surface was extremely slippery and in some places oil, brake fluid, and anti-freeze residue was present on the track, which was especially noticeable during wetness.

Of course, I cannot be responsible for your actions. It would be the same as saying, "Go ahead and jump off the 30 m[2] bridge and nothing will happen to you." You have to watch out for yourself!

About the sketches: They are to provide you with an orientation of the track layout. The sketches are in no way drawn to scale. When looking at the track from Google Earth via satellite, everything looks fairly boring as does the "drawn to scale" sketches in Ulrich Thomson's driver handbook. The track width does not correspond to the track length. There is no action in view!

The sketches in this book were drawn in a way so the rider will see them at recorded speed. The curves race towards you and become extremely narrow; the speed changes the perspective. I compared the satellite track contour with my sketches, and they are similar. The difference lies in the eyes of an experienced Nordschleife professional. For this reason, I drew my sketches in more detail to clearly point out the important areas.

The photographs that I used here were taken during a bicycle tour; therefore, you will see a few bicyclists. I photographed from one section to the next portraying the entire track without a gap. A free video showing the pictures in motion is available at: www.nürburgring.de. Today it is forbidden to photograph or film the track.

[1]Negligent suicide: Recklessly endangering your own life, resulting in death.
[2]1 Meter = 3.281 feet

The sketches of the track are displayed from the bottom to the top, just like the photographs, from the bottom to the top. When the book lies in front of you, you will notice that the track "moves away" from you. The arrow located on the side indicates the driving direction. Located on the right page are the photographs, each one marked with a number, displaying the direction of the track, and also the corresponding view to that section of the track.

The given speeds are suggested values! They are based on a 75 kg (165 lbs.)[1] rider on an FZR 1000, manufactured in 1988, with Bridgestone BT 57 tires, and an outside temperature of 20 – 28 °C (68 – 84 F°)[2]. The speeds can be achieved only when the line is correct!

In the end, what really matters is that you have an exact mental image of the track! The order is as follows: studying, riding, studying, riding, studying, riding, riding, riding, a brief review, riding, riding, riding, etc. To just watch the video will not be of much benefit to you. The sketches with the given speeds and the individual photographs are more important.

After studying the book, and you're on the track, say the upcoming track section, so that you know where you are, and so that you can activate the images you put into memory. In Ulrich Thomson's driver handbook for the Nürburgring Nordschleife, Helmut Dähne drew "the ideal line." This of course does not work. It was the ideal line for Helmut Dähne on a Honda RC 30.

Every motorcycle has a different line due to its weight, its acceleration, its braking ability, and the rider. It is understandable that someone who weighs 50 kg (110 lbs.) will brake later than someone weighing 100 kg (220 lbs.). As mentioned earlier, there are riders with different styles, again resulting in a different line. But lines are similar.

My experience on the subject line is: Line results in speed, and every additional movement requires time and utilizes speed. A line should be a harmonic process with as little movement as possible! Ripping the throttle and a hectic acceleration will cause commotion in the bike. It would be better to treat your bike like a raw egg, with calmness and composure.

I never intended to make this book available to the general public. Neither the photographs nor the sketches have professional status; they were intended for home use as a tool in order for me to understand "The Green Hell." The photographs were taken with an old Canon T 70 during a bicycle tour event on the Nordschleife.

I invested a great deal of time and effort in the material. The negatives were sent in and digitized to DVD with the best possible resolution and then added to the book. Therefore, be somewhat lenient when judging the photographs in the book.

This book is intended for the rider to provide him with more safety!

[1] 1 Kilogram (kg) = 2.205 pounds (lbs.)
[2] Tc (temperature in degrees Celsius) = (TF-32) / 1.8

Start on Döttinger Höhe

You start on the Döttinger Höhe, and as a pro you know that the tires are still cold; therefore, ride the first lap slowly. It is also a good idea to stop at the ticket office and inquire about the latest track conditions, e.g., accidents, oil spills, etc. Keep in mind: You are riding the "Green Hell," and parts of it go through forest, which could be wet.

I believe I no longer have to describe how to ride a curve - from the outside to the inside, keeping in mind the course of the next curve, or even the one after that.

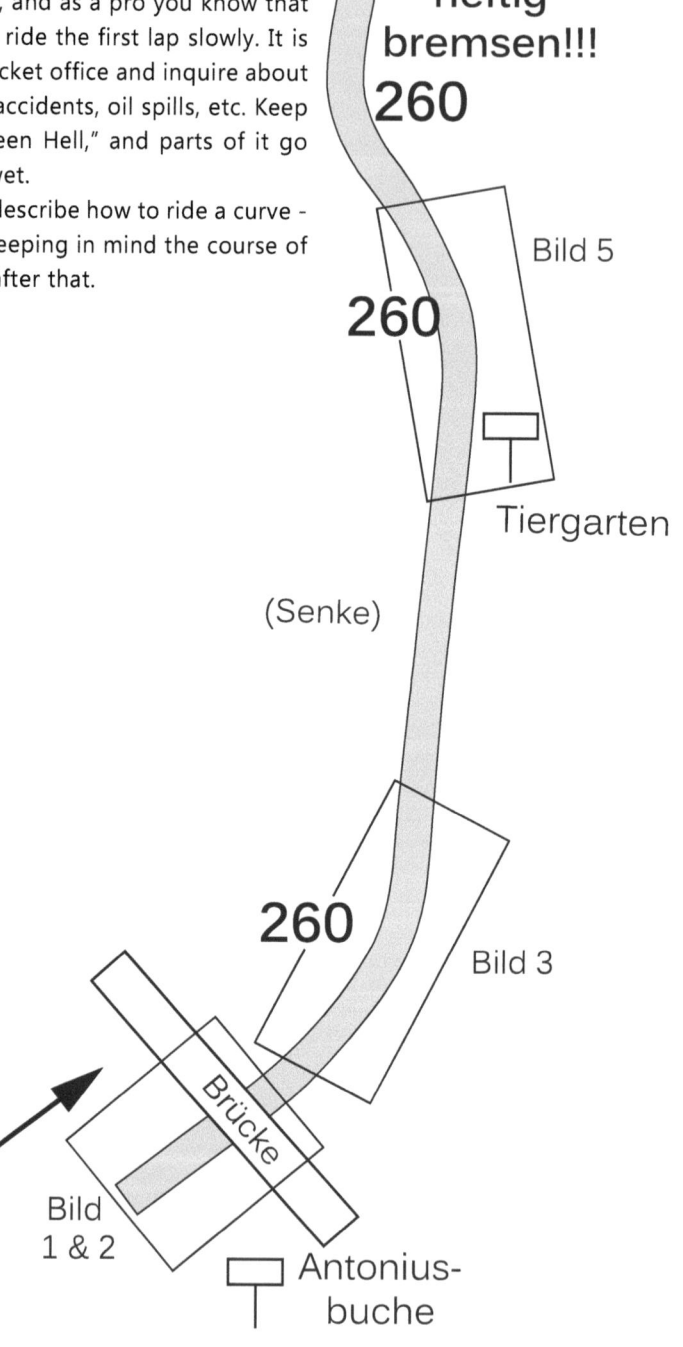

heftig
bremsen!!!
260

260

Bild 5

Tiergarten

(Senke)

260

Bild 3

Brücke

Bild
1 & 2

Antonius-
buche

Bild 5

Bild 3

Bild 4

Bild 1

Bild 2

Tiergarten to alte Boxengasse
In photograph 6, you are braking to the fullest extent!

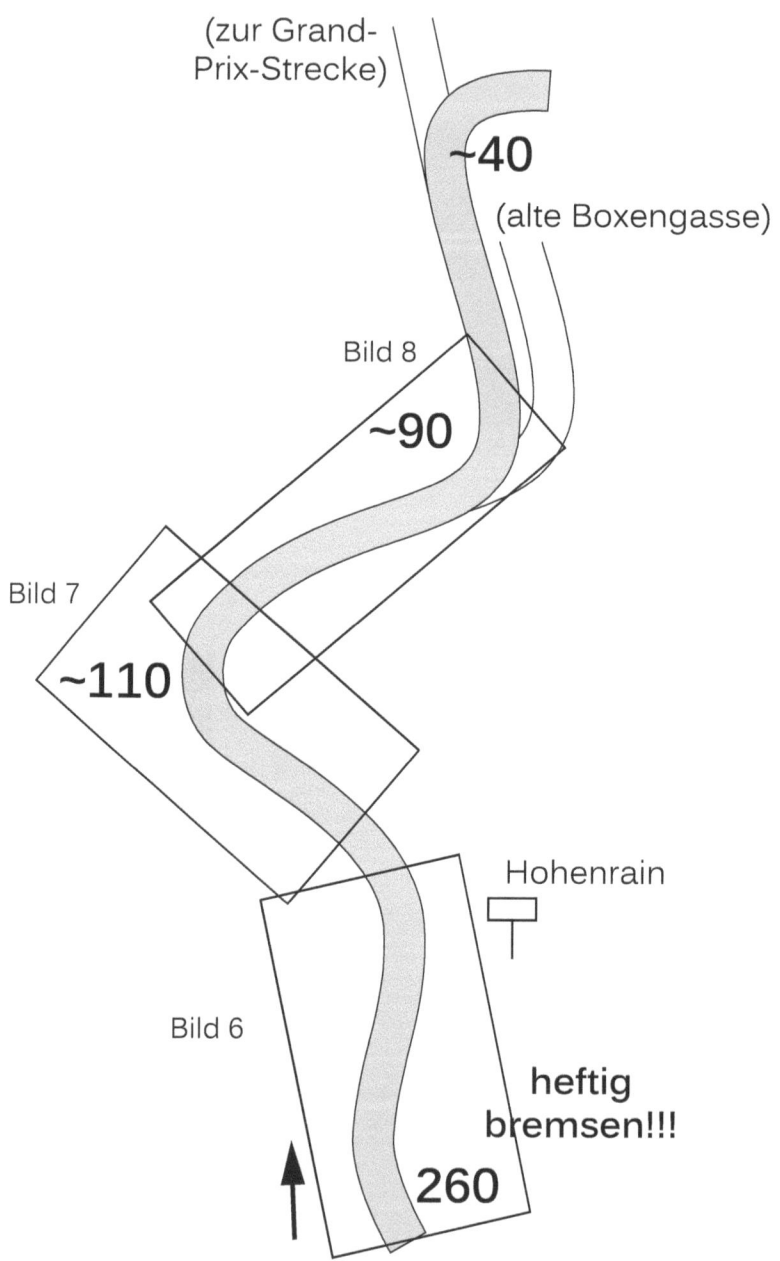

(zur Grand-Prix-Strecke)

~40

(alte Boxengasse)

Bild 8

~90

Bild 7

~110

Hohenrain

Bild 6

heftig bremsen!!!

260

Bild 8

Bild 7

Bild 6

Exit Alte Boxengasse to Entrance Hatzenbach

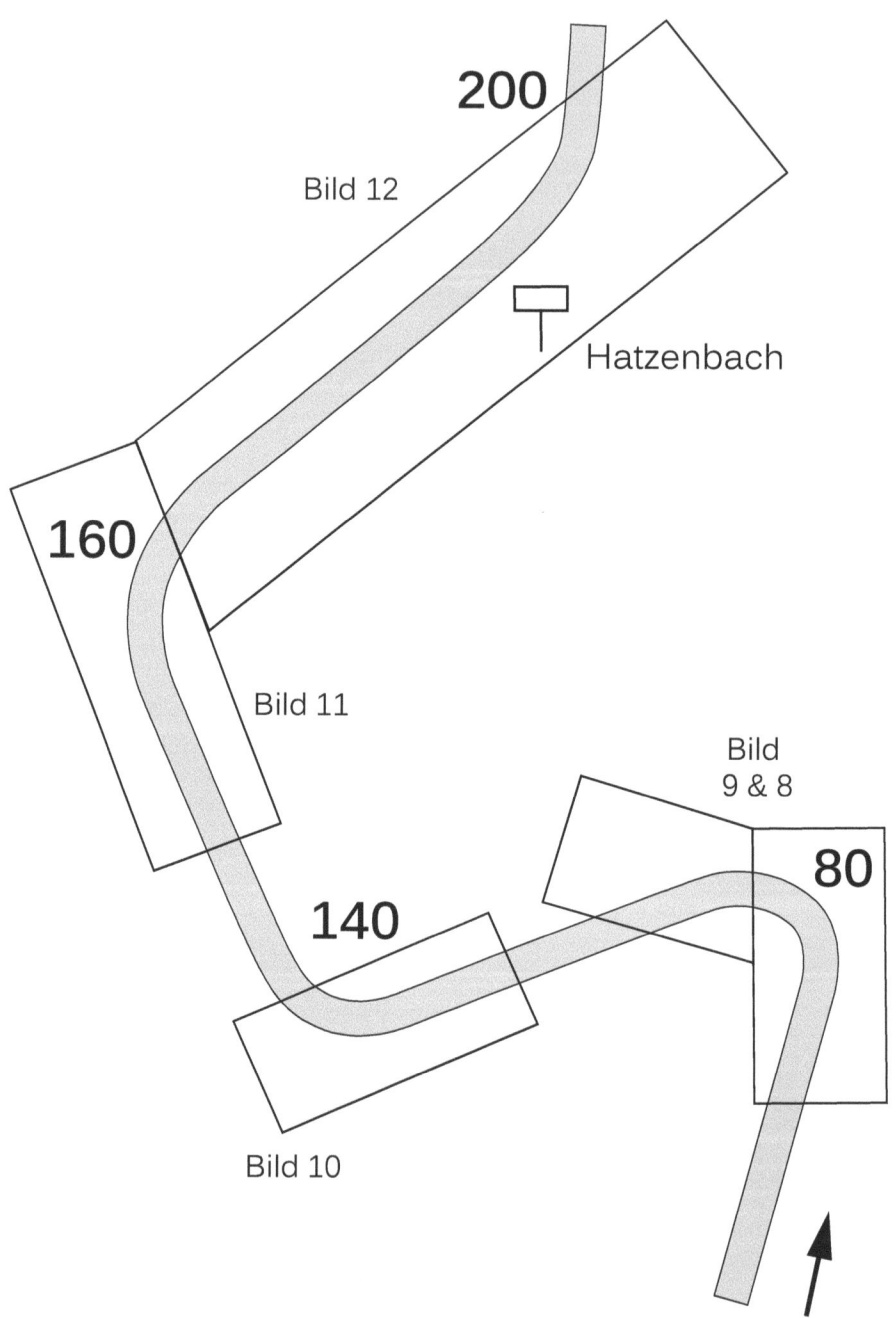

200

Bild 12

Hatzenbach

160

Bild 11

Bild
9 & 8

80

140

Bild 10

Bild 12

Bild 10

Bild 11

Bild 8

Bild 9

Hatzenbach

Since you are a late braker, you will try to ride the easy left in photograph 14 in an almost straight line while braking.

At the cross, you release the brake, angling the motorcycle to the right. It is not a nice line, but you are damn fast! In order to ride "an ideal line," you will have to brake much earlier.

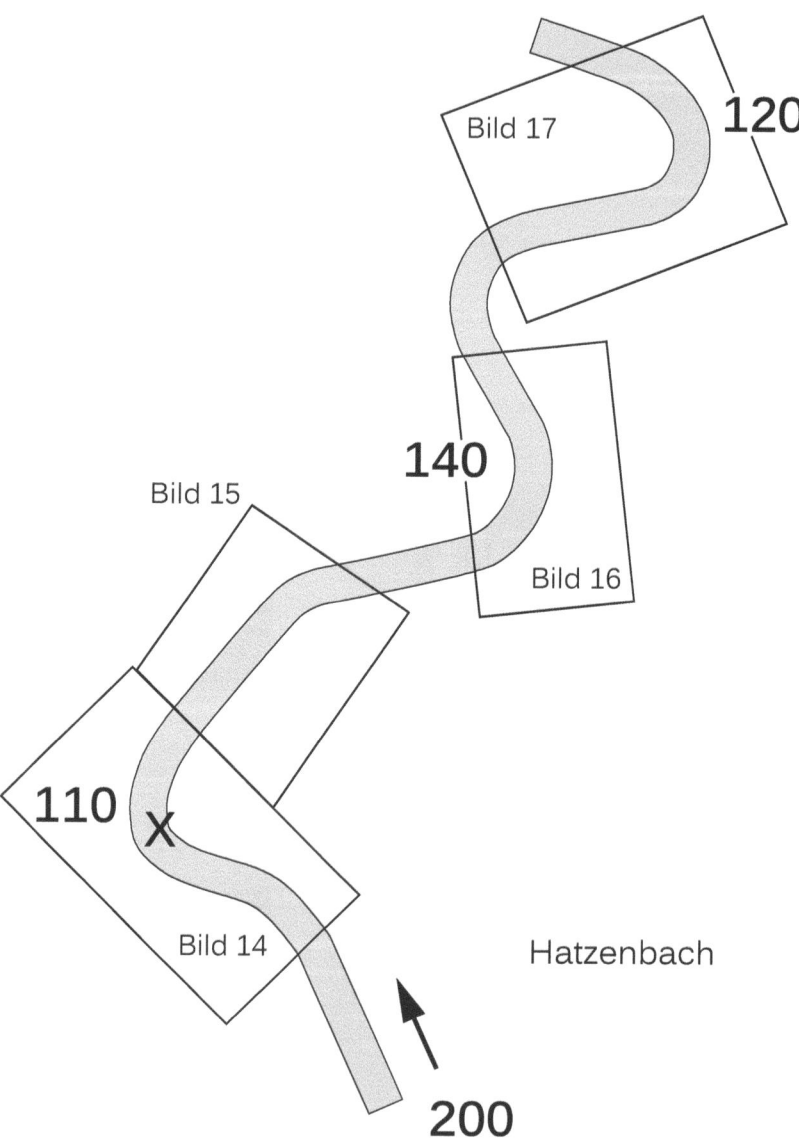

Hatzenbach

Bild 17

Bild 15

Bild 16

Bild 13

Bild 14

Hocheichen to Quiddelbacher-Höhe

Hocheichen is a corkscrew curve. Consider a fairly late lean, as it will narrow a bit at the end. CAUTION! You're riding downhill and the weight of the motorcycle is pushing forward.

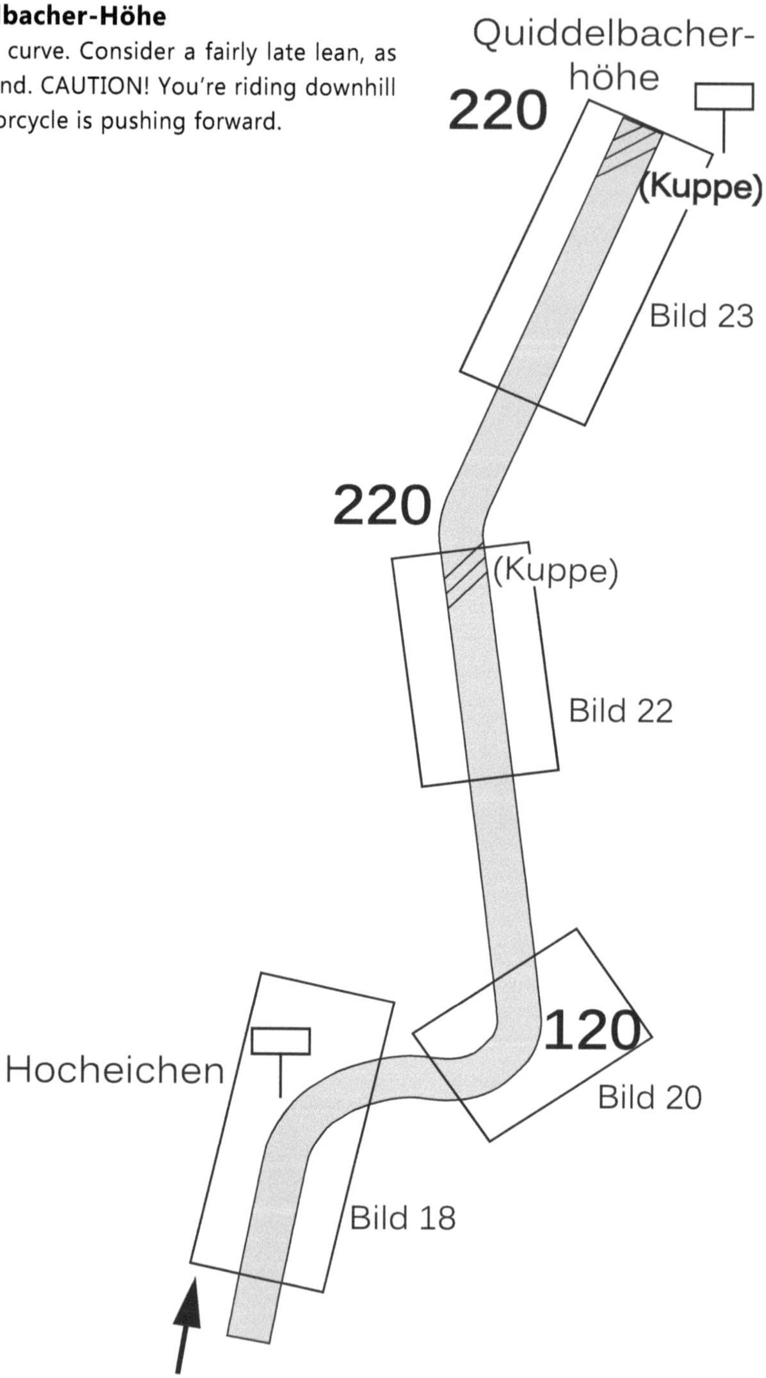

Quiddelbacher-höhe

220

(Kuppe)

Bild 23

220

(Kuppe)

Bild 22

120

Bild 20

Hocheichen

Bild 18

Bild 22

Bild 23

Bild 20

Bild 21

Bild 18

Bild 19

Quiddelbacher Höhe and Flugplatz

Approaching Quiddelbacher Höhe: At this speed you will in fact lose the road. CAUTION! If you're too fast you will be unable to take the upcoming right. See photograph 25. This is where Manfred Winkelhock flipped over backwards in a Formula 2 car.

The following double right, photographs 25 – 27, can be ridden in one arc. Afterward, continue with full throttle.

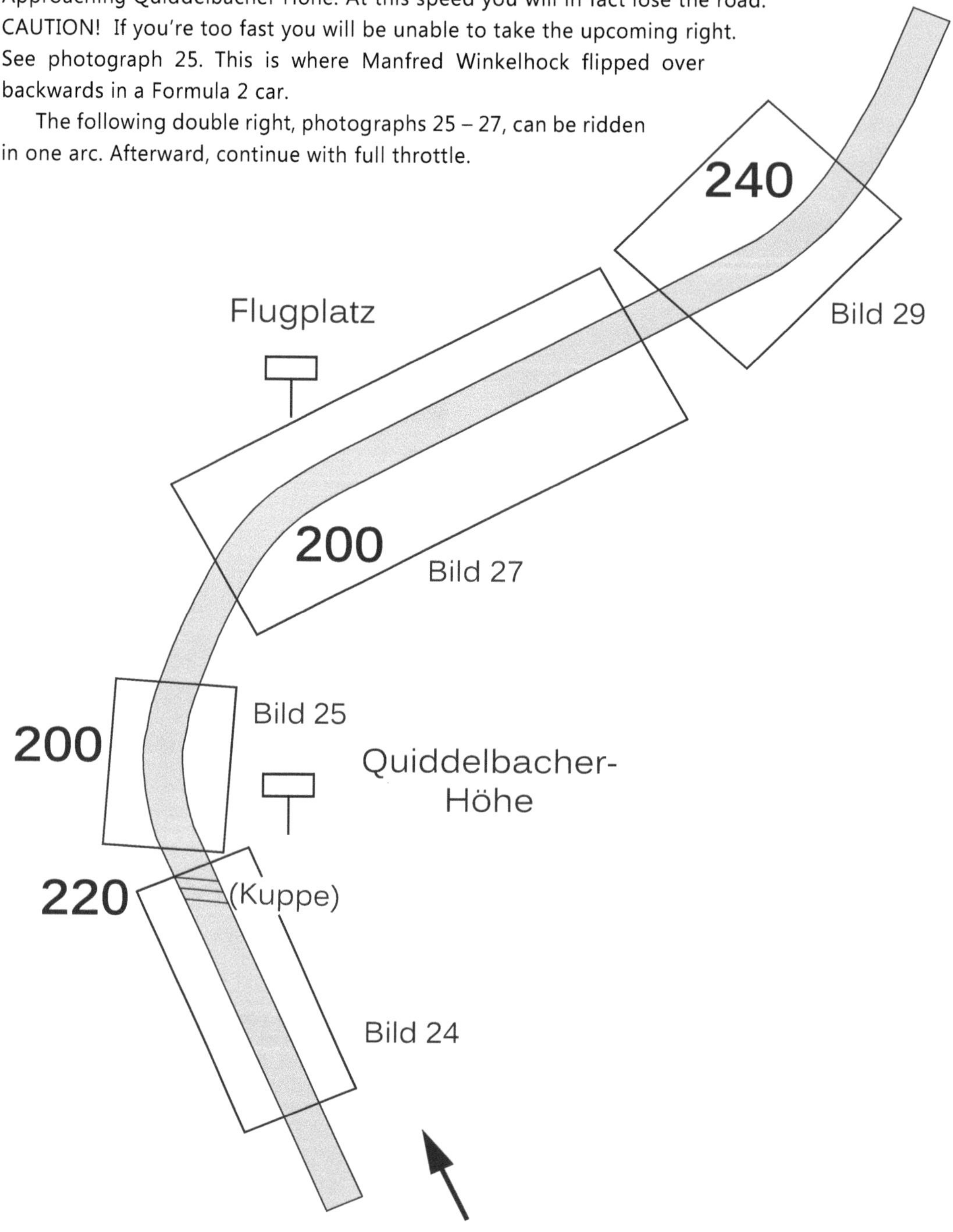

240

Bild 29

Flugplatz

200

Bild 27

Bild 25

200

Quiddelbacher-
Höhe

220 (Kuppe)

Bild 24

Bild 28

Bild 29

Bild 26

Bild 27

Bild 24

Bild 25

Schwedenkreuz

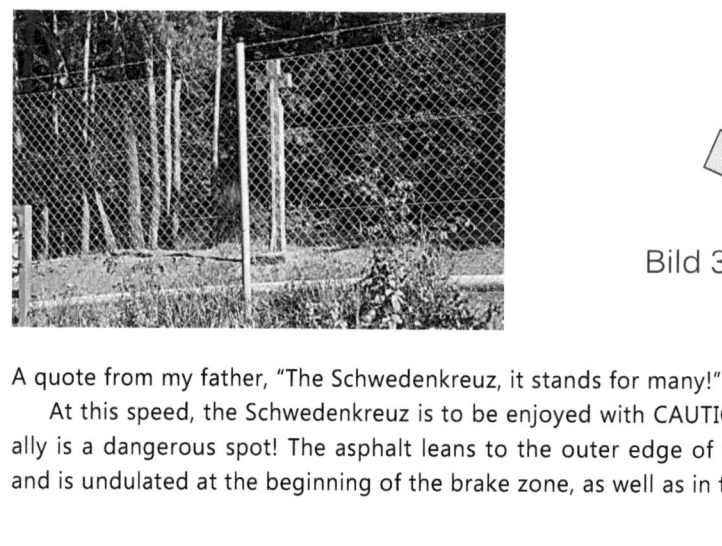

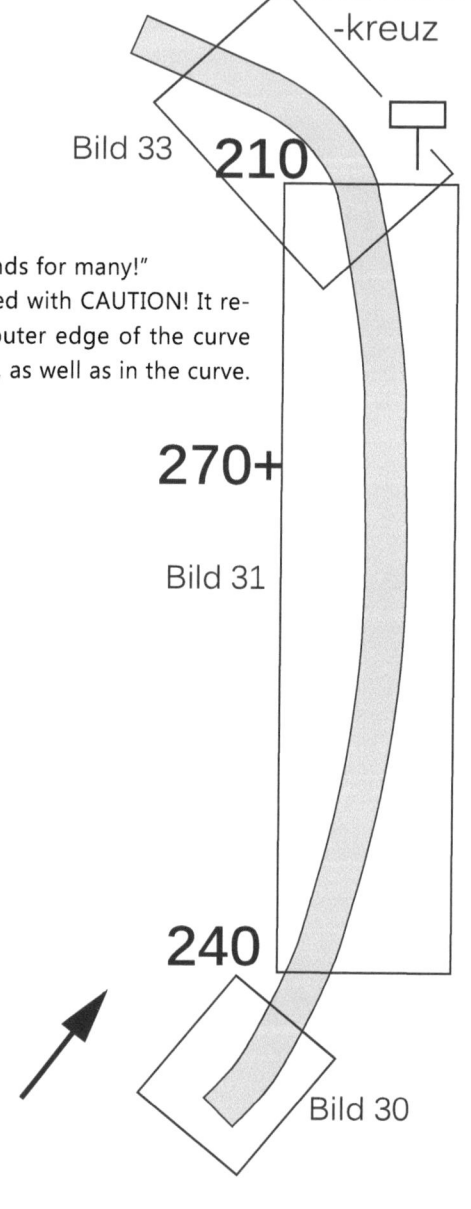

Schweden-kreuz

Bild 33

210

270+

Bild 31

240

Bild 30

A quote from my father, "The Schwedenkreuz, it stands for many!"

At this speed, the Schwedenkreuz is to be enjoyed with CAUTION! It really is a dangerous spot! The asphalt leans to the outer edge of the curve and is undulated at the beginning of the brake zone, as well as in the curve.

Bild 33

Bild 32

Bild 31

Bild 30

Arembergkurve

Photograph 34 displays the approach to the Arembergkurve. It is an unobstructed view.

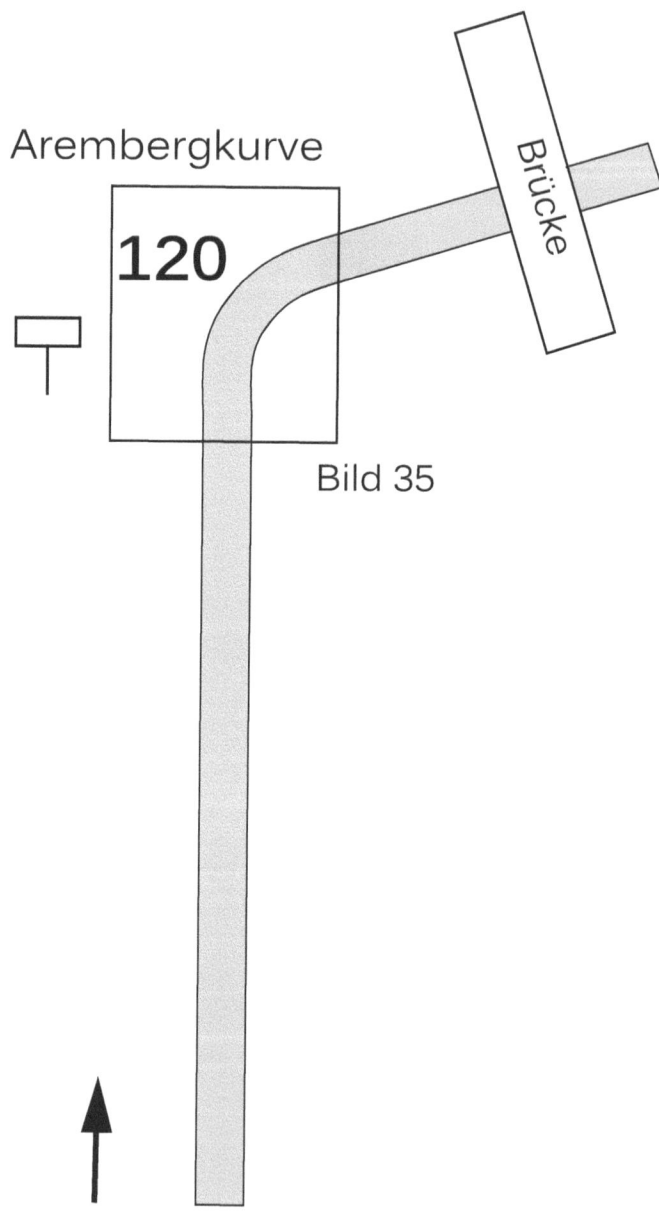

Arembergkurve

120

Brücke

Bild 35

Bild 36

Bild 35

Bild 34

Fuchsröhre

After the Arembergkurve, you can ride the motorcycle in a straight line downhill through the small curves of the Fuchsröhre with the throttle at full blast.

At this point, you're getting really fast and you might not have enough strength to maintain an upright torso position due to the downward G-force when you're flying through the dip in the Fuchsröhre at 270 km/h (169 mph).

You must brake at the spot where the bicyclist is shown in photograph 41 in order to make the next left at 210 km/h (131 mph).

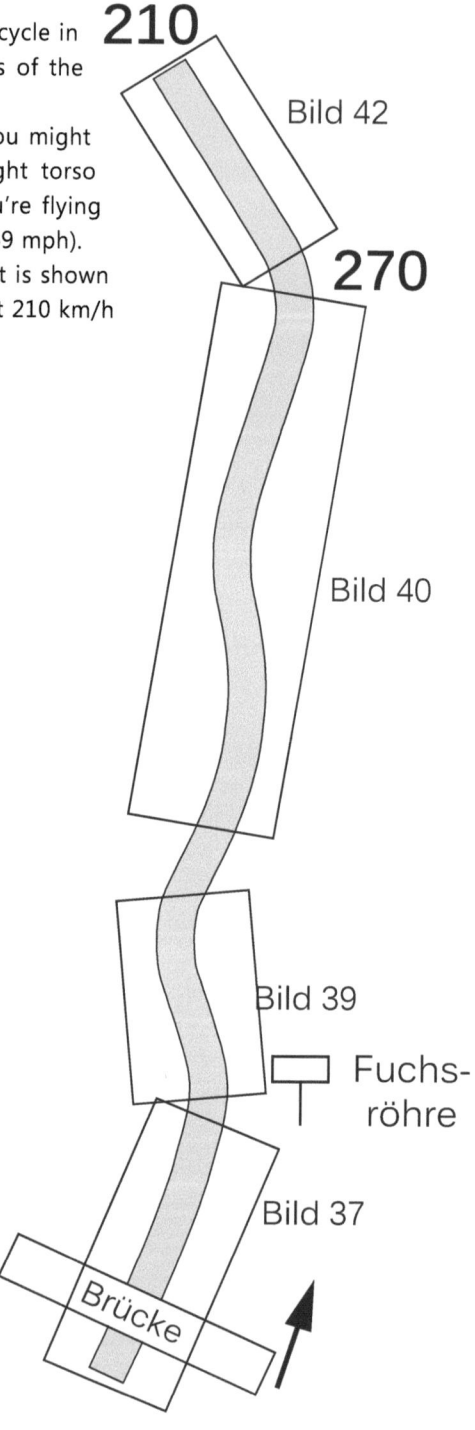

Bild 41

Bild 42

Bild 39

Bild 40

Bild 37

Bild 38

Adenauer Forst

Be aware, most misfortunes happen at the Adenauer Forst. Up until now, everything is going well, but coming up the road there are now many tire marks, and then, all of a sudden, the road is gone! See photograph 46. Exercise CAUTION at the hairpin turn coming up after the knoll!

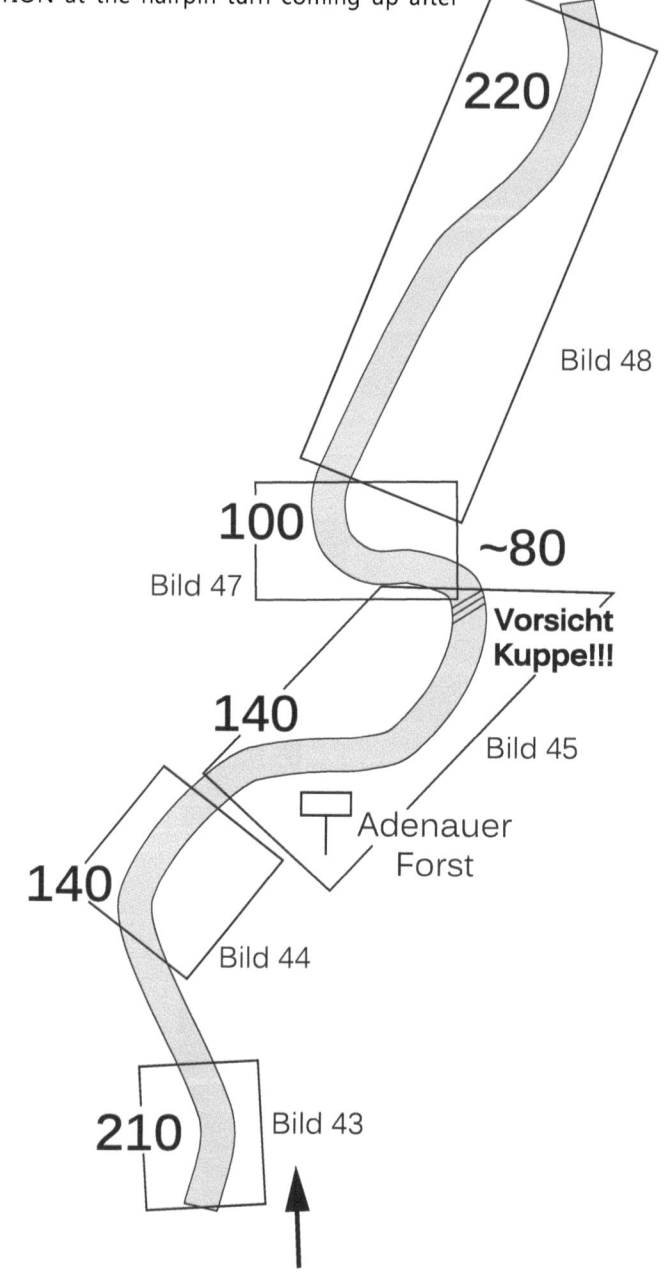

220

Bild 48

100

Bild 47

~80

Vorsicht Kuppe!!!

140

Bild 45

140

Adenauer Forst

Bild 44

210

Bild 43

Bild 47

Bild 48

Bild 45

Bild 46

Bild 43

Bild 44

Metzgesfeld

The first left, depicted in photographs 50 and 51, is a bit scary and extremely fast, but the surface has sufficient grip. The second left again is to be approached with CAUTION, as it will narrow toward the end.

Passing over the knoll, it is now downhill to Kallenhard .

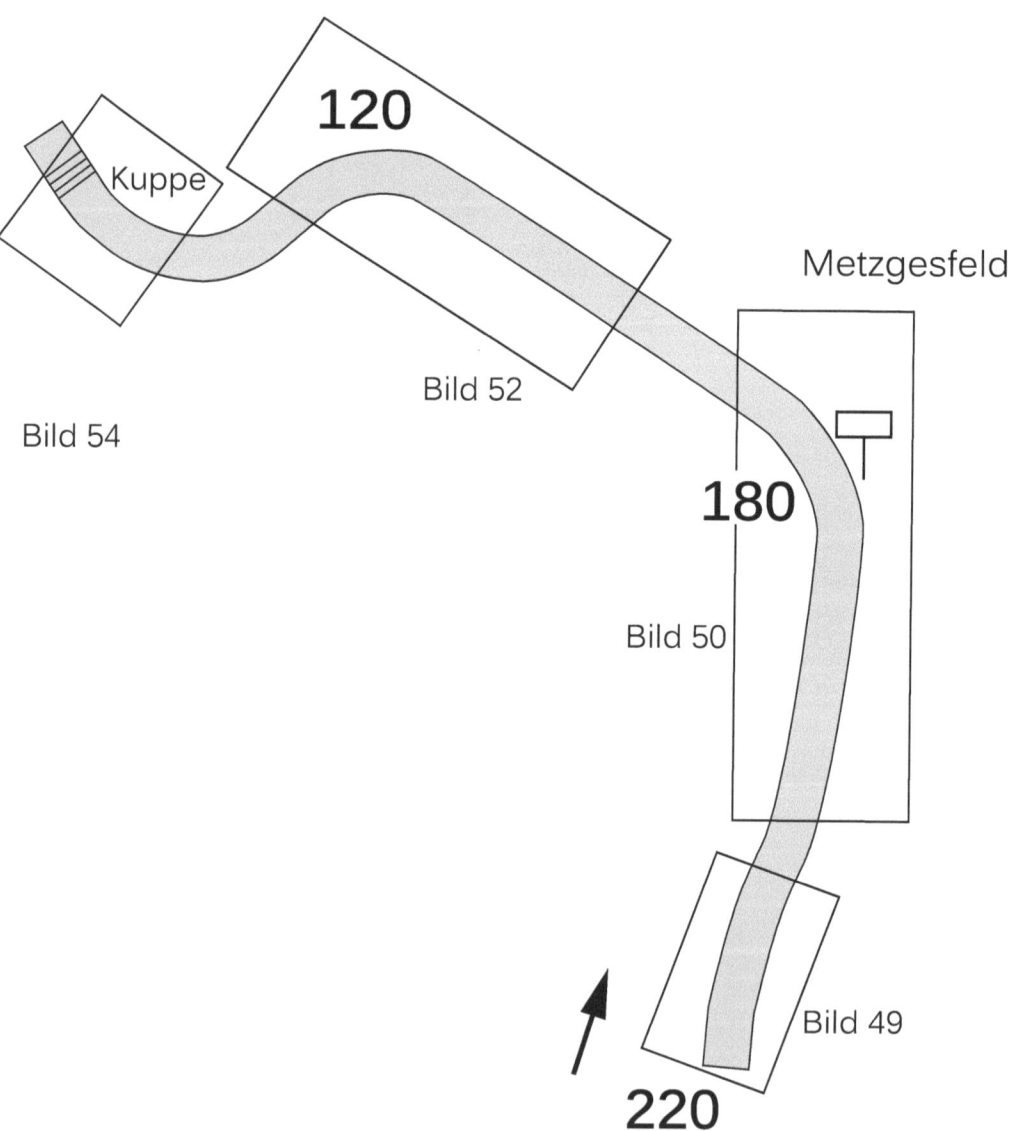

Bild 53

Bild 51

Bild 52

Bild 49

Bild 50

Kallenhard

Kallenhard is a bit undulating; the following chicane requires some guts!

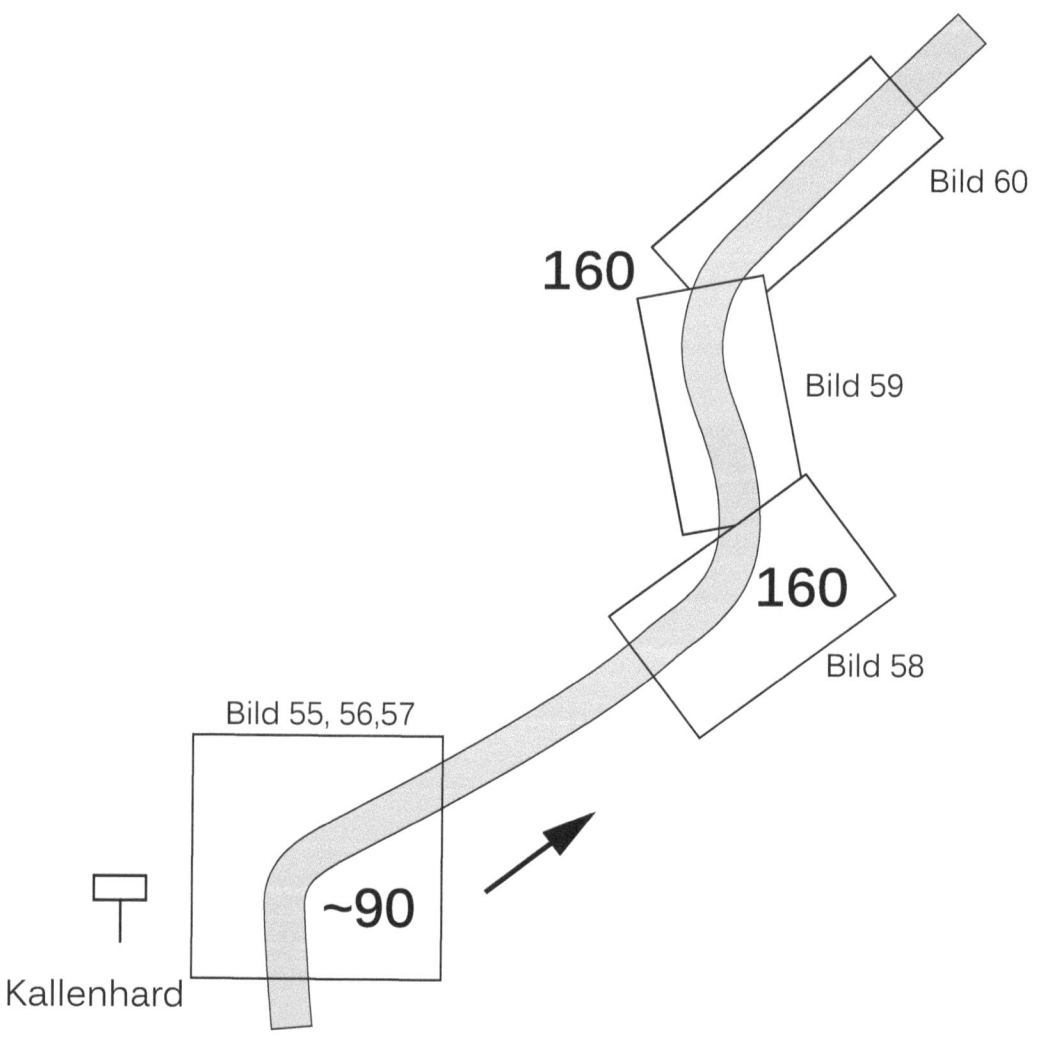

Bild 60

160

Bild 59

160

Bild 58

Bild 55, 56,57

~90

Kallenhard

Bild 59

Bild 60

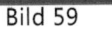

Bild 57

Bild 58

Bild 55

Bild 56

Wehrseifen

The triple right is also a bit faster. At Wehrseifen, there are riders who like to ride an extra loop. As a late braker, you repeat the riding maneuver like Entrance Hatzenbach and continue braking into the Wehrseifen, then lean the bike to the left at the cross.

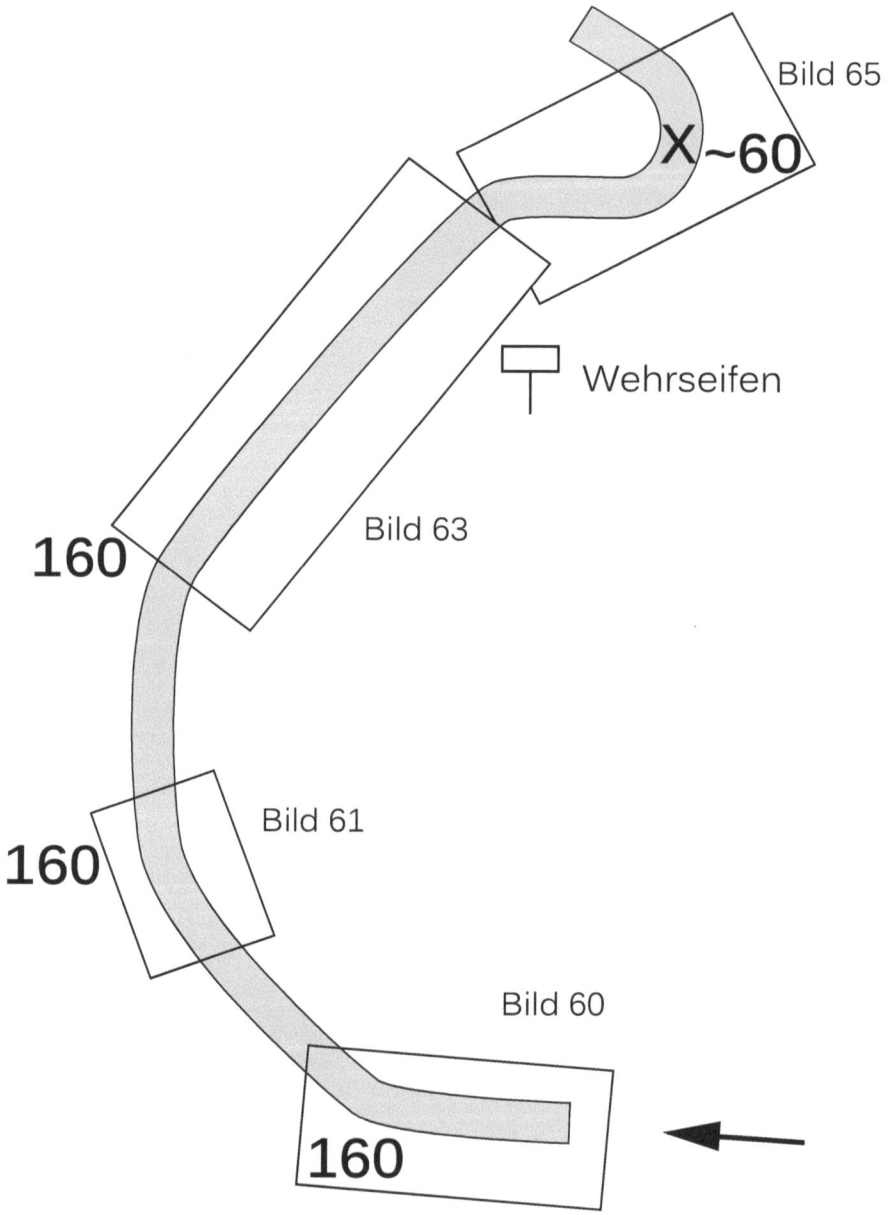

Bild 65

X ~60

Wehrseifen

160

Bild 63

Bild 61

160

Bild 60

160

Bild 64

Bild 65

Bild 62

Bild 63

Bild 60

Bild 61

Access Breidscheid

With increasing speed, you can accelerate out of Wehrseifen. But hey! *You* have to figure out the braking point in Breitscheid before the first left. As indicated, every motorcycle has a different braking point according to the characteristics of the bike and the weight of the rider. Wanting to be really fast on the Nordschleife, you must know how to reduce the speed of the bike by applying the brakes, which requires you to estimate the braking distance.

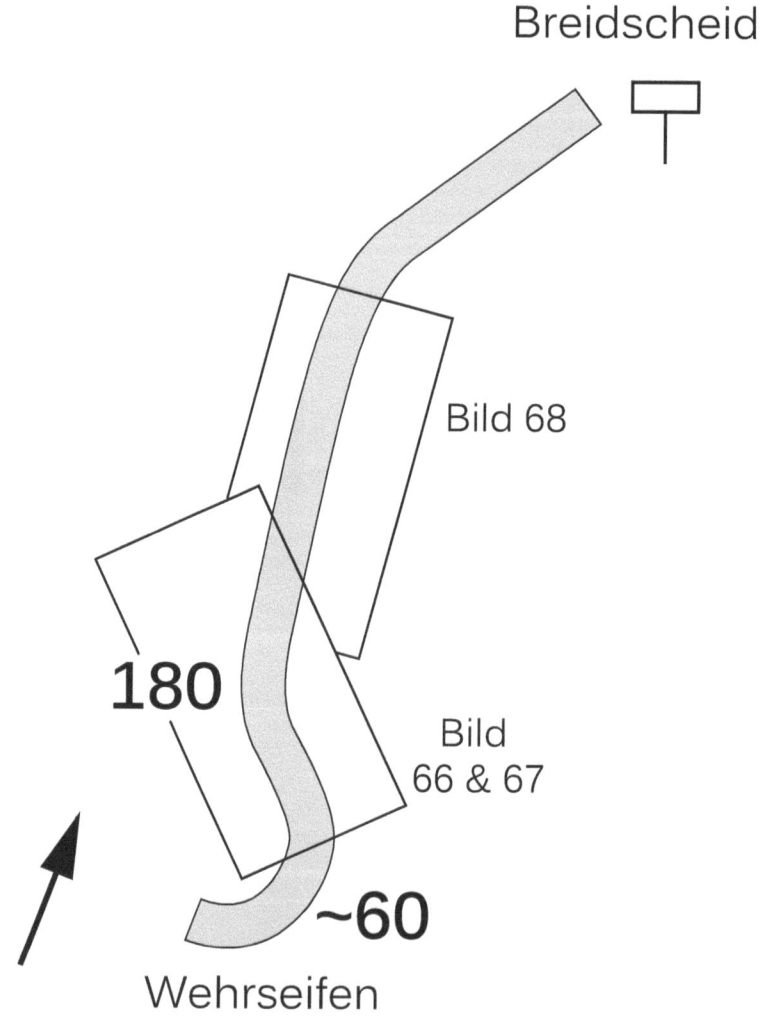

Bild 68

Bild 67

Bild 66

Breidscheid to Exmühle

Descend to Breidscheid is a wicked double left. ☺
The second left, an elegant radius with increasing speed, is a bit faster.
CAUTION! At Exmühle, the track is somewhat uneven and easily closes in..

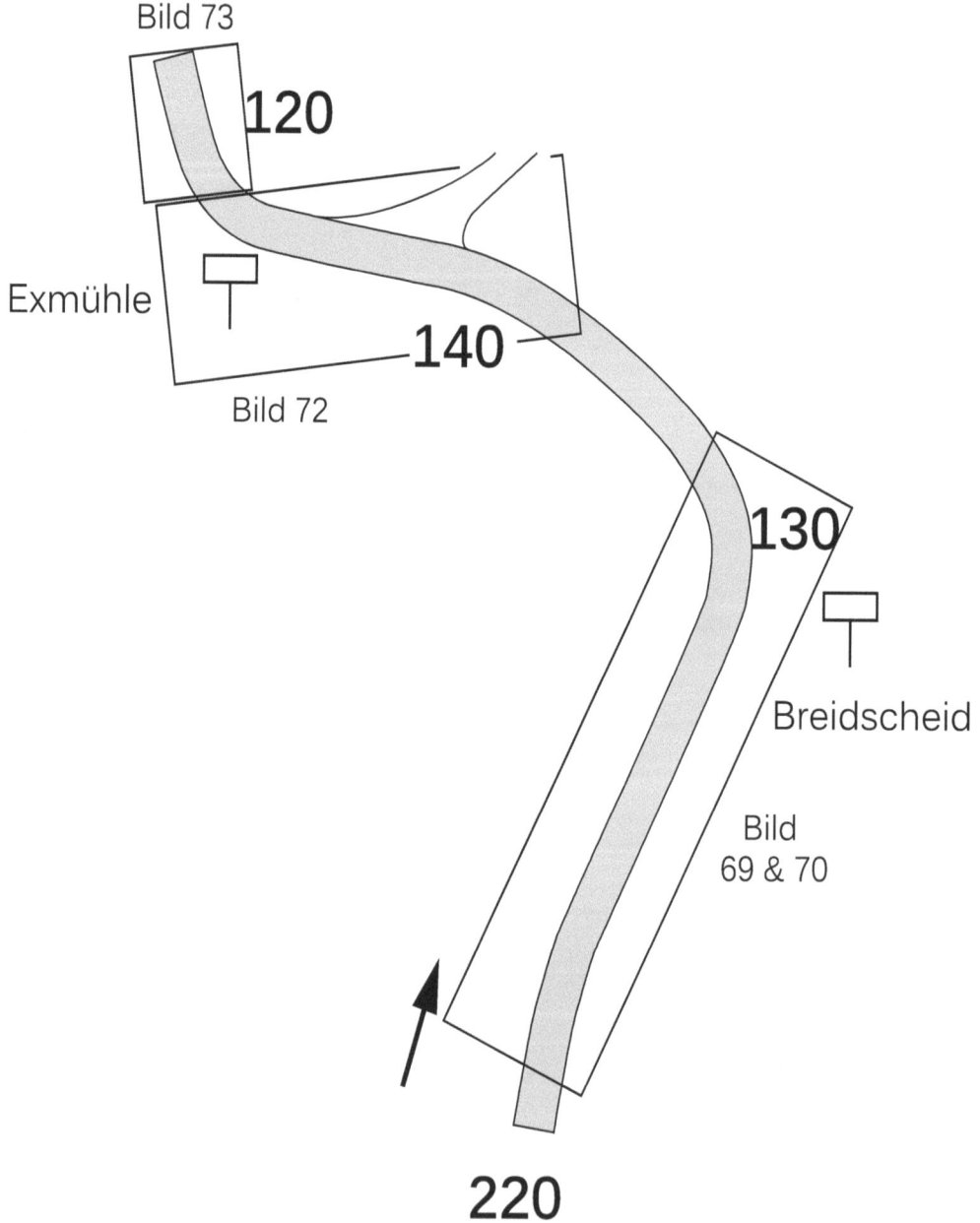

Bild 73

120

Exmühle

140

Bild 72

130

Breidscheid

Bild
69 & 70

220

Bild 73

Bild 71

Bild 72

Bild 69

Bild 70

Bergwerk

When exiting Exmühle, accelerate! Pictured in photograph 75 is the Niki Lauda Left. This is where the old champion had his almost fatal accident.

After the left, reduce the throttle and brake heavily; otherwise, the Bergwerk will be impossible. Steer into the Bergwerk quite a bit later, at the beginning of the triple planked crash barrier. When I started riding the Nordschleife, the Bergwerk seemed like a never-ending curve to me, and it required some practice on my part.

"Flying blind" means a lot of mental work!

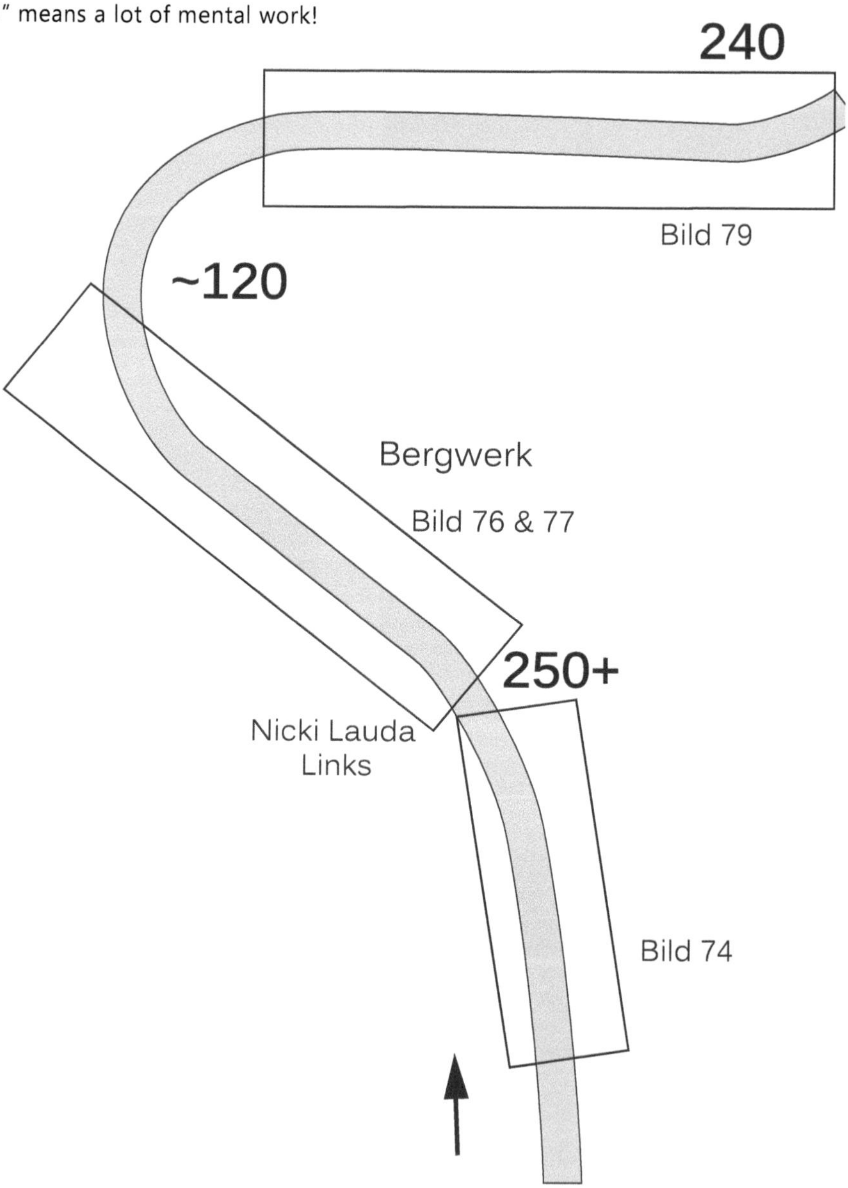

240

Bild 79

~120

Bergwerk

Bild 76 & 77

250+

Nicki Lauda Links

Bild 74

Bild 78

Bild 79

Bild 76

Bild 77

Bild 74

Bild 75

At Access Kesselchen

This is where the knowledge of the track pays off - mostly obstructed areas at a high speed!

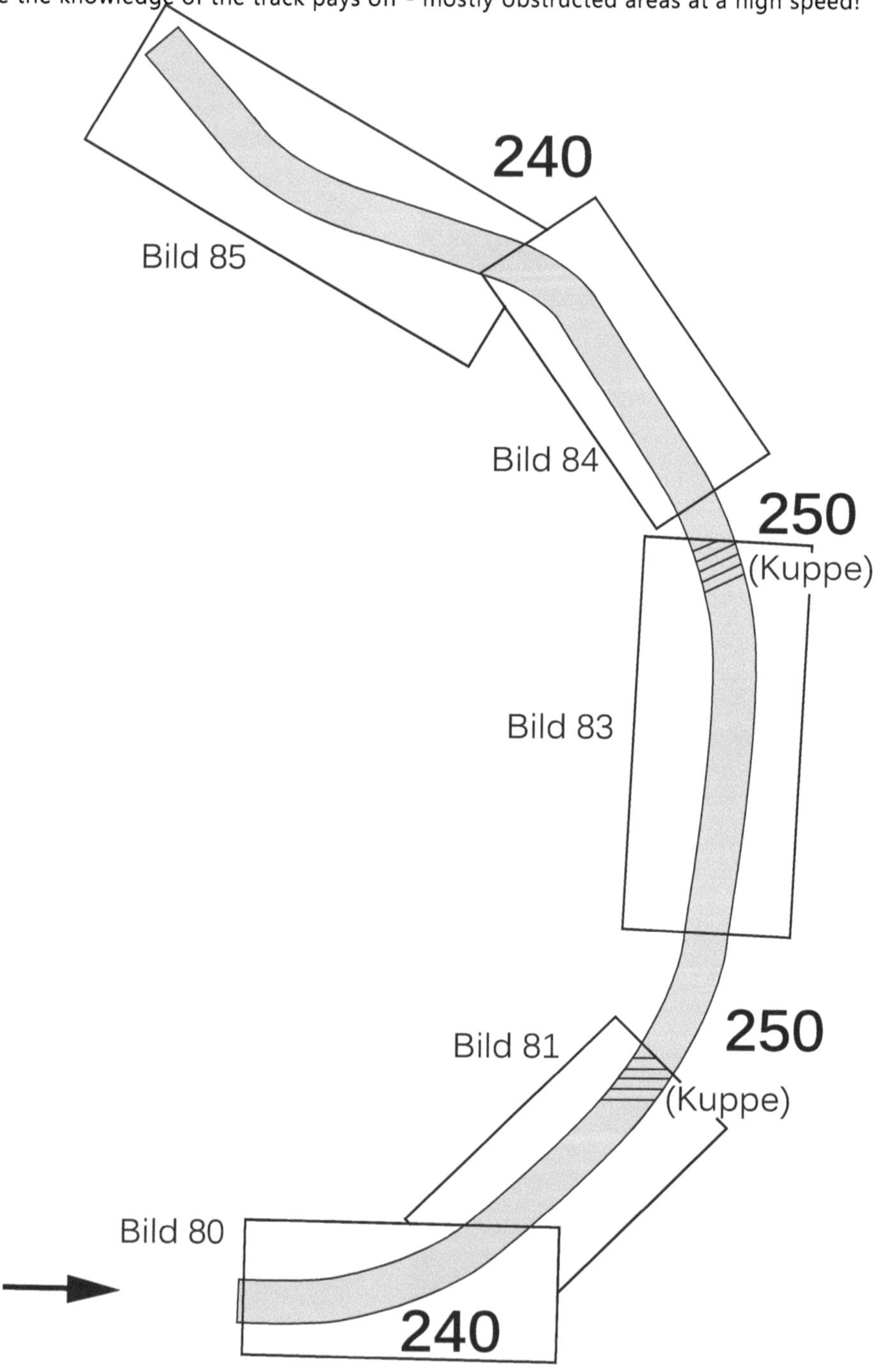

240

Bild 85

Bild 84

250
(Kuppe)

Bild 83

250
(Kuppe)

Bild 81

Bild 80

240

Bild 84

Bild 85

Bild 82

Bild 83

Bild 80

Bild 81

Kesselchen

One of the fastest sections of the loop. There is a strong ascent that you are barely aware of with the motorcycle; however, I noticed it when I rode it on the bicycle.

The left, shown in photographs 89 and 90 closes in a bit; therefore, reduce your speed..

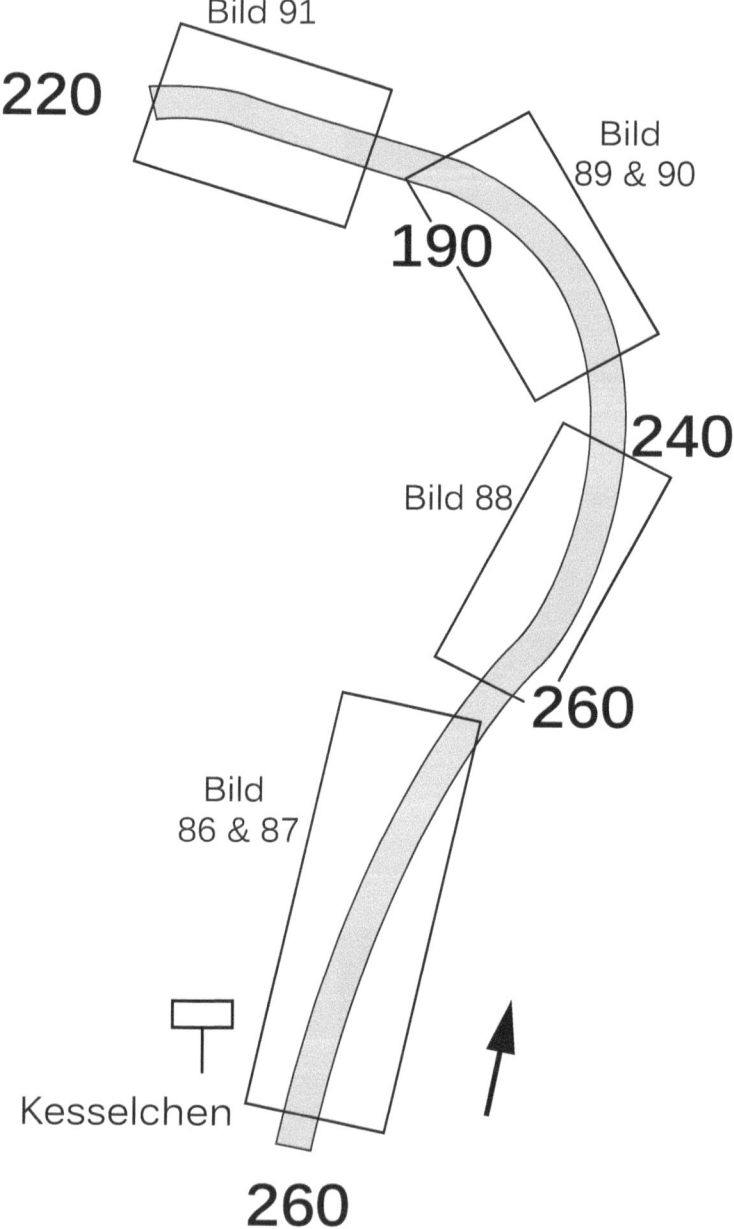

Bild 90

Bild 91

Bild 88

Bild 89

Bild 86

Bild 87

Ausgang Kesselchen und Klostertal

After the knoll, refer to photograph 92. Take the right with low throttle, since the tires don't have full contact with the road. Approaching Klostertal at the dip, photograph 95, the tires again will have a decreased contact with the track – remain calm.

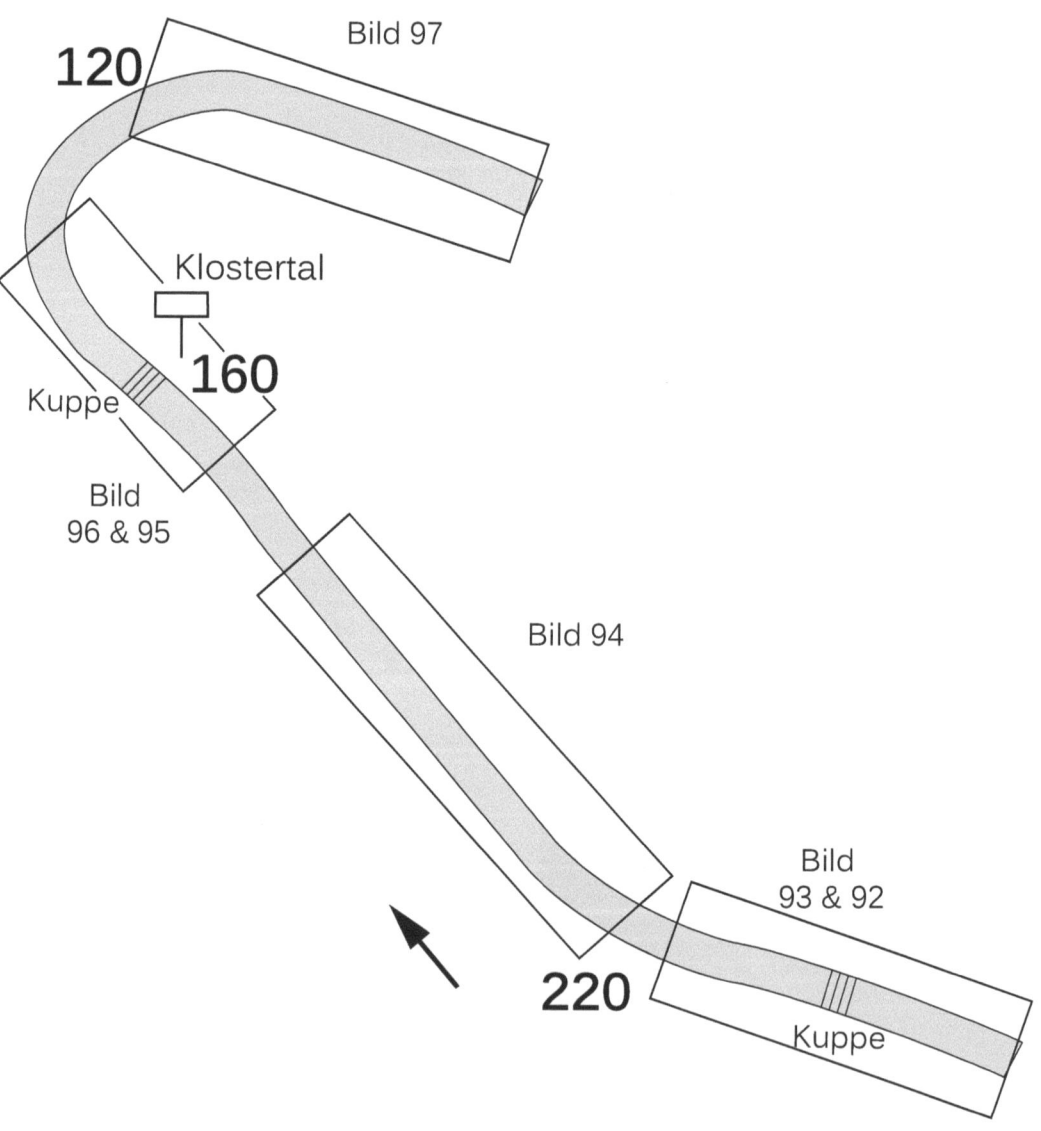

Bild 96

Bild 97

Bild 94

Bild 95

Bild 92

Bild 93

Karussell

Now we're going up to the Karusell. You almost leap into the oval with its concrete slabs - to be exact, the second slab. Now this means remaining in the oval. Due to the high compression, the foot pegs easily scrape the track. CAUTION! Ride the steep curve to the end, otherwise the angle of the slabs will act like a "ski-jump." Doing 220 km/h (137 mph) in photograph 102 takes a lot of guts! And that goes without saying. ☺

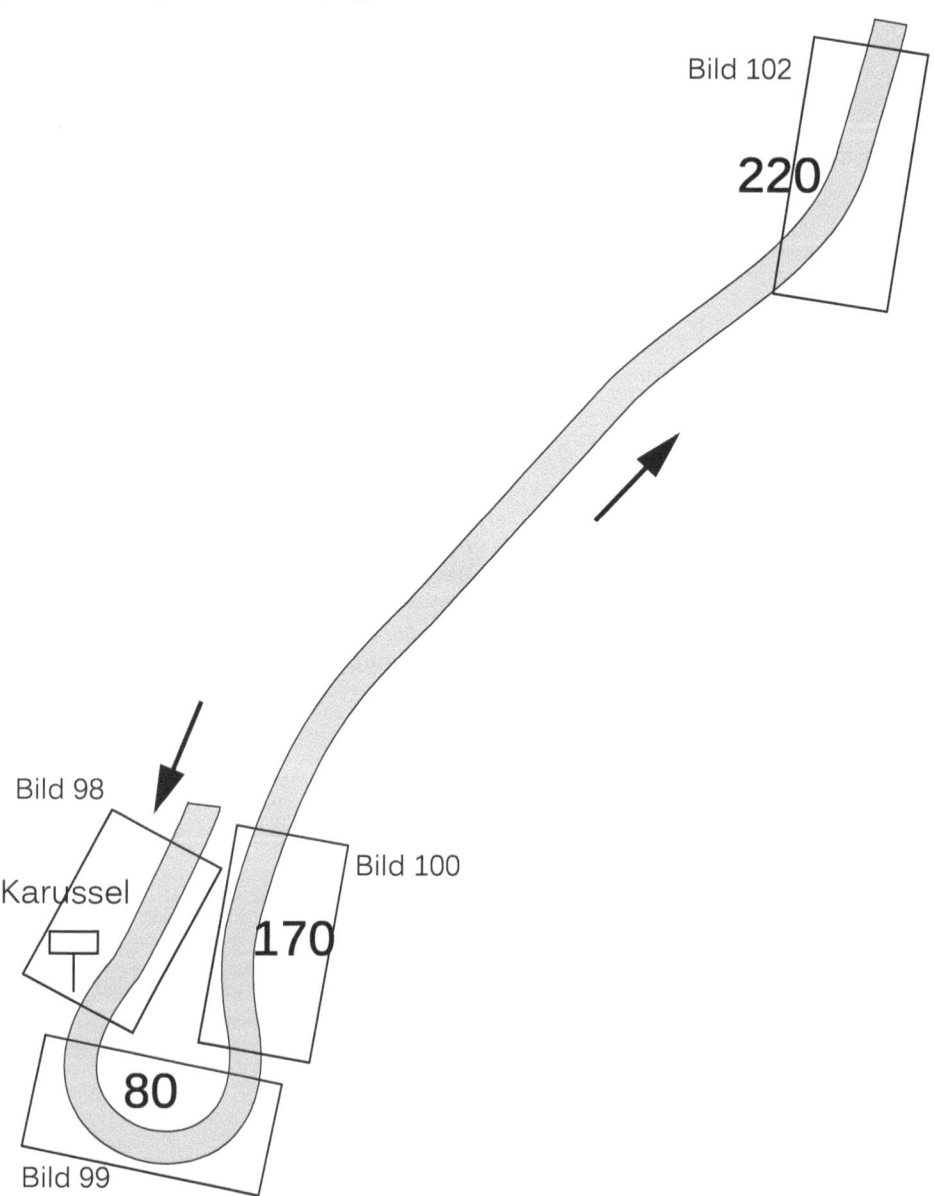

Bild 102

Bild 100

Bild 101

Bild 98

Bild 99

Hohe Acht and Hedwigshöhe

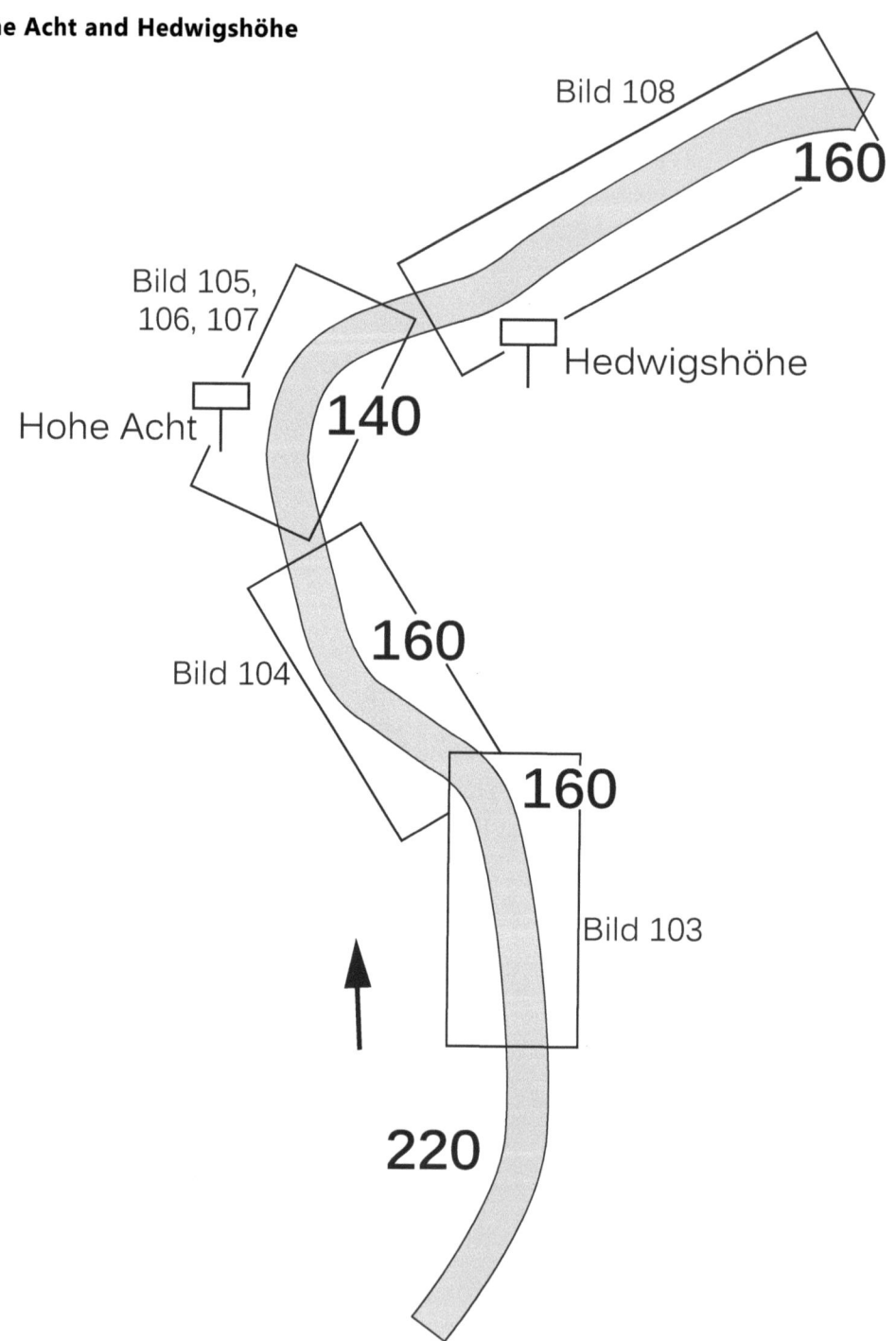

Bild 108

160

Bild 105,
106, 107

Hedwigshöhe

Hohe Acht

140

160

Bild 104

160

Bild 103

220

Bild 107

Bild 108

Bild 105

Bild 106

Bild 103

Bild 104

Wippermann and Eschbach

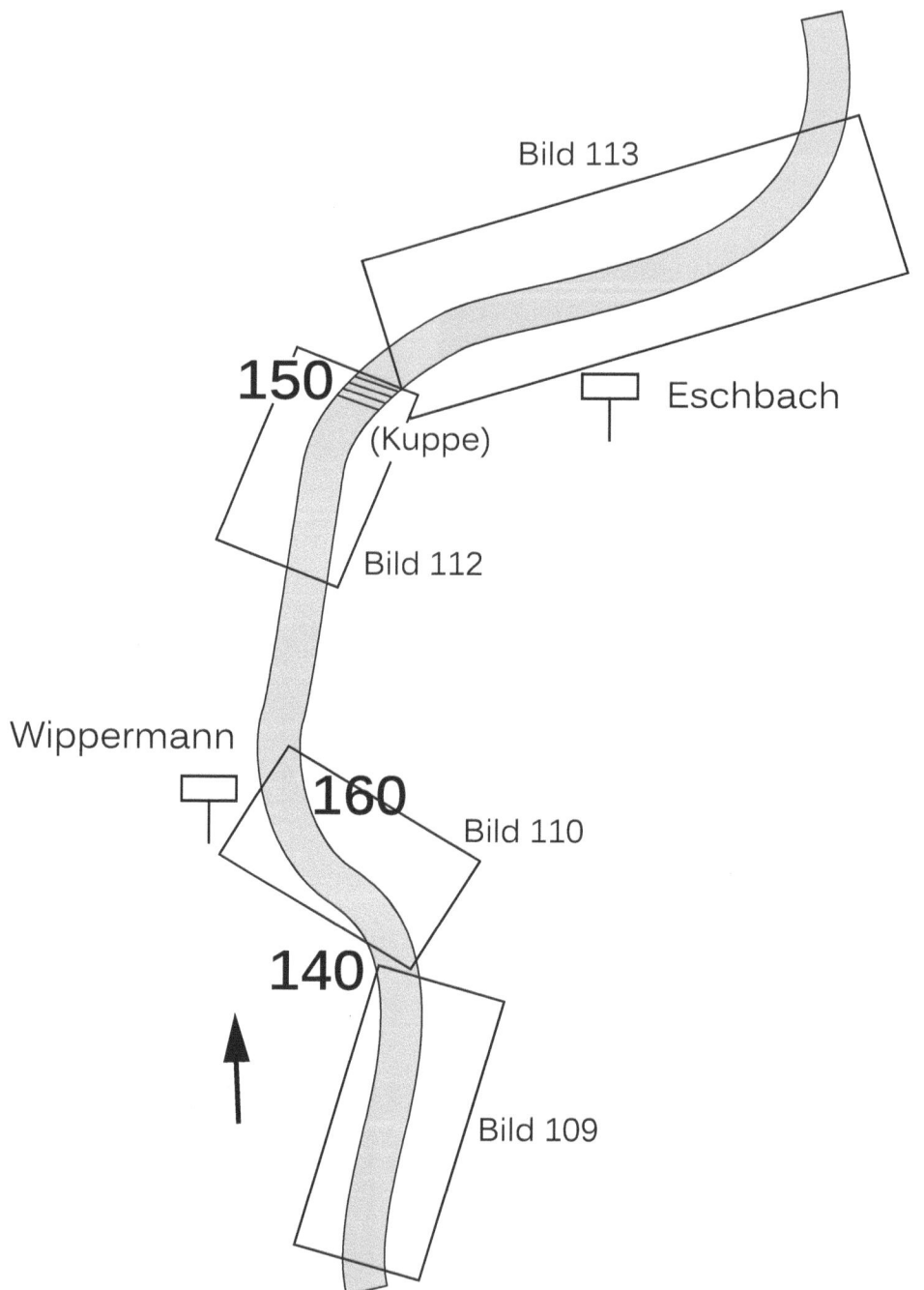

Bild 113

150
(Kuppe)

Eschbach

Bild 112

Wippermann

160

Bild 110

140

Bild 109

Bild 113

Bild 111

Bild 112

Bild 109

Bild 110

Brünnchen

Exercise CAUTION in approaching the right, see photograph 116, entering Brünnchen. This is a descent, and you will notice how the weight of the motorcycle can cause it to wander outward.

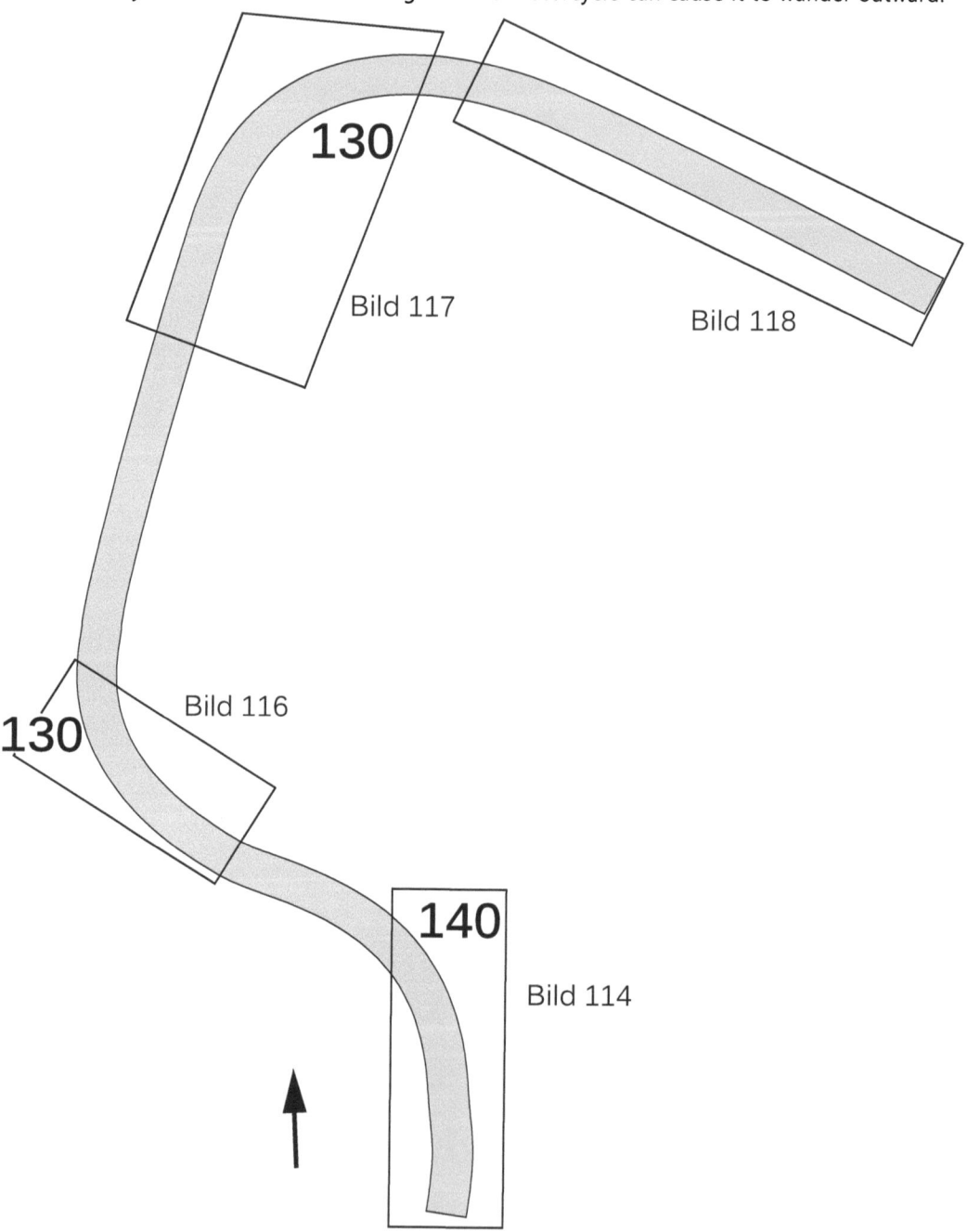

130

Bild 117

Bild 118

Bild 116

130

140

Bild 114

Bild 118

Bild 116

Bild 117

Bild 114

Bild 115

Eiskurve to Pflanzgarten

On top of the knoll, photograph 122, both wheels will lose contact with the ground. Ride the double right, photograph 123, in an arc.

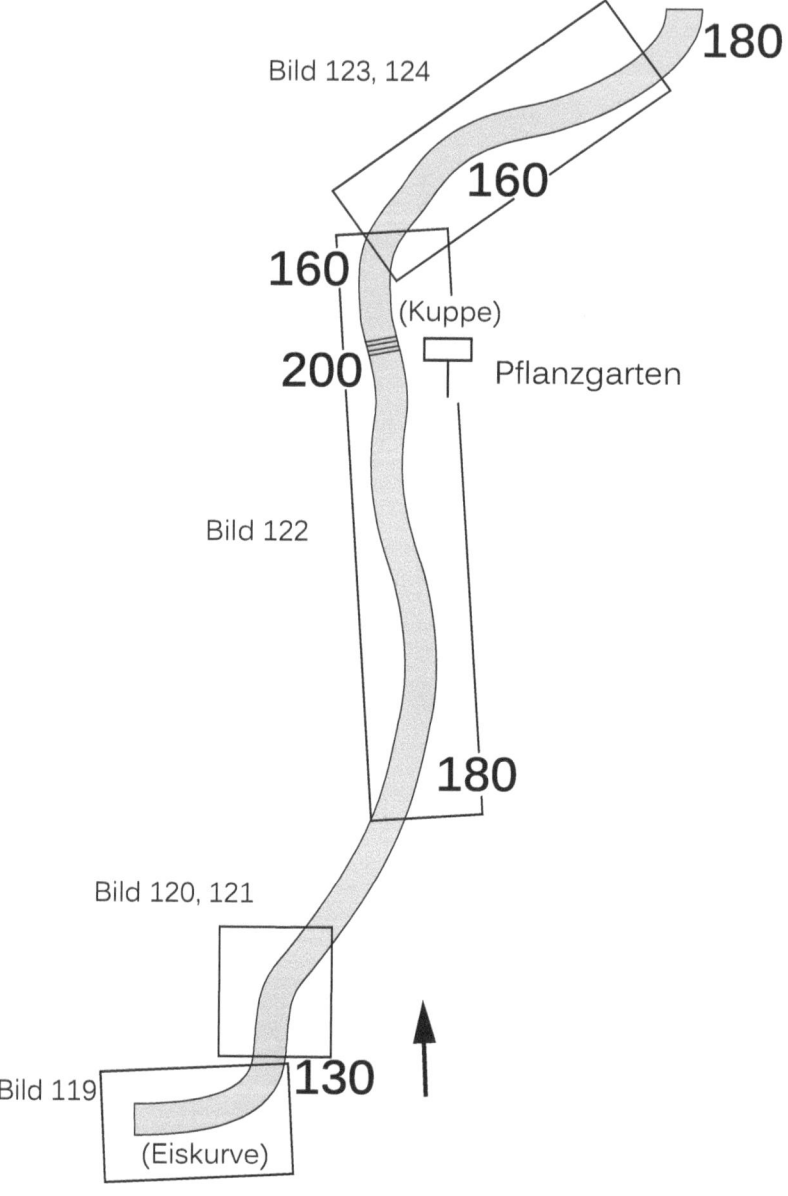

Bild 123, 124

180

160

160

(Kuppe)

200

Pflanzgarten

Bild 122

180

Bild 120, 121

Bild 119

130

(Eiskurve)

Bild 123

Bild 124

Bild 121

Bild 122

Bild 119

Bild 120

Pflanzgarten

Approach the knoll, photograph 125, slowly and with CAUTION. The front wheel will become very light.

Also, use CAUTION at the knoll, photograph 127! I once tried it at 220 km/h (137 mph) and sustained a vertebrae injury that resulted in a 10-day hospital stay at Adenau.

This right-left-right combination can be executed closely along the curbs almost in a straight line. The surface of the right curve, photograph 129, at the end of the straight has become a bit undulated.

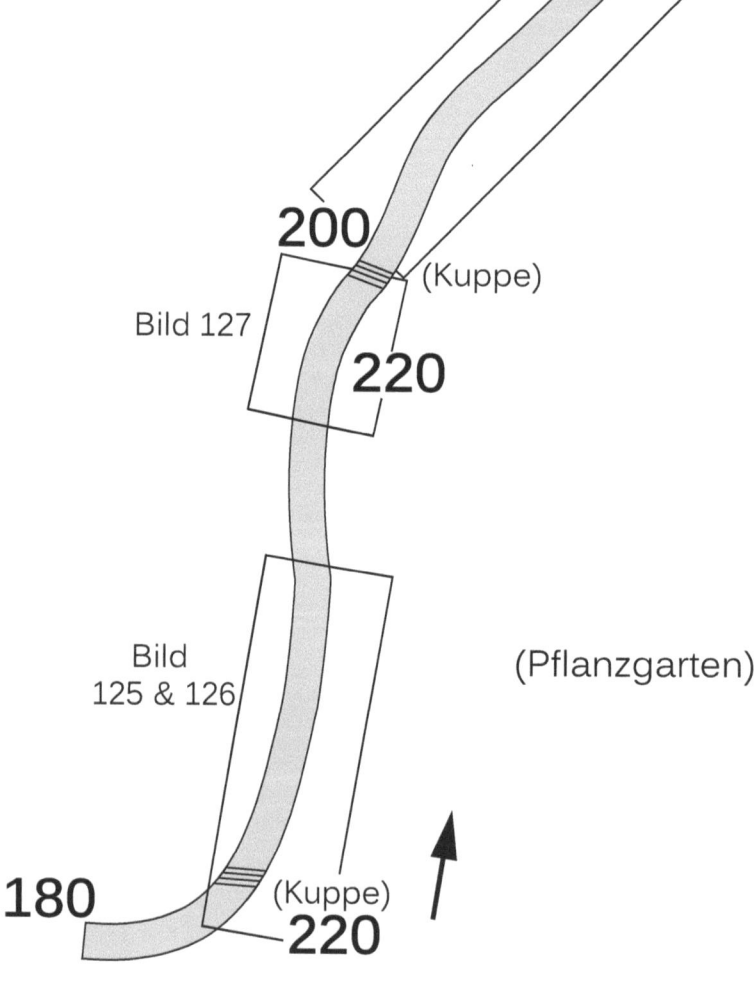

200

Bild 128 & 129

200

(Kuppe)

Bild 127

220

Bild 125 & 126

(Pflanzgarten)

180

(Kuppe)

220

Bild 129

Bild 130

Bild 127

Bild 128

Bild 125

Bild 126

Entrance Schwalbenschwanz, Galgenkopf to Döttinger Höhe

CAUTION, the left, photograph 131, is sharper than you think. It is a small hairpin turn, which narrows towards the end. The entrance to Schwalbenschwanz is completed in a lean by crossing over the first right concrete slab. Here the same concept applies as with the Karusell, remain low until the end!

Ride through the double right of the Galgenkopf in an arc accelerating while exiting, as it will open up at the end. Some practice is necessary when figuring out the arc at the Galgenkopf.

Accelerate at the center of the first bend to the right, while keeping in mind the bike's performance and reducing the speed before the vertex of the second bend. Utilize the Döttinger Höhe to ride slow, so that the brakes and the engine can cool down.

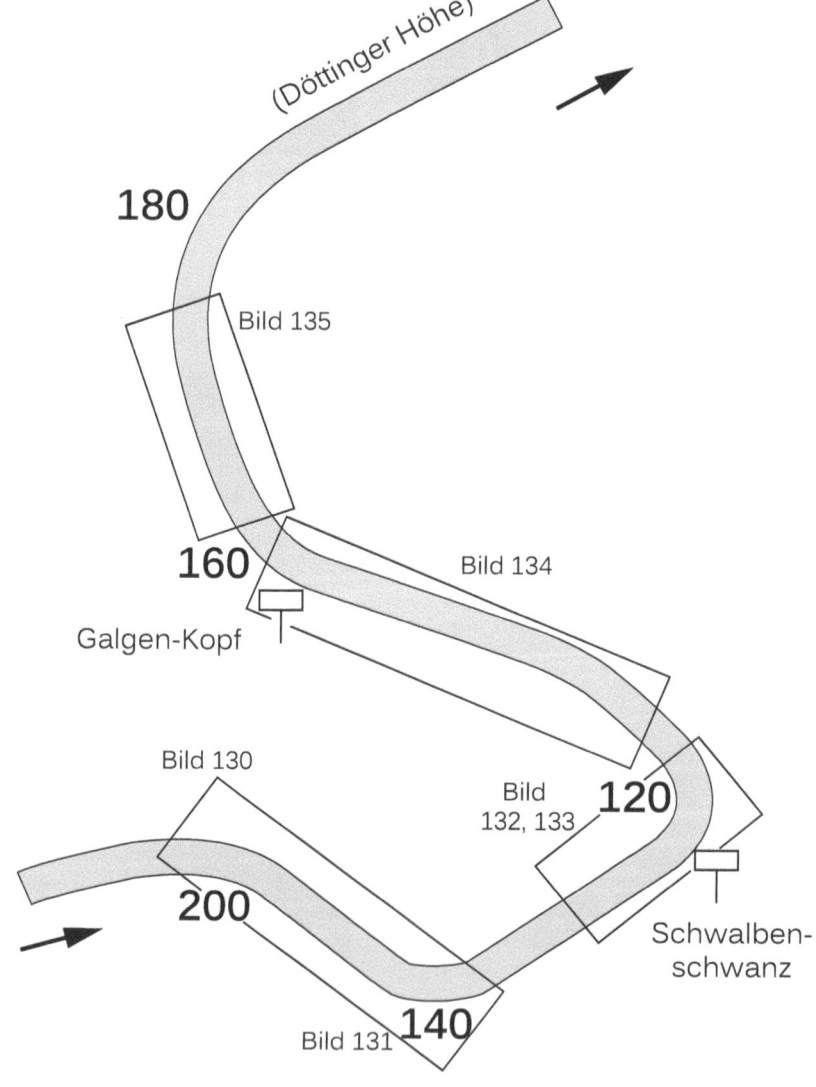

Bild 134

Bild 135

Bild 132

Bild 133

Bild 130

Bild 131

Closing remarks

Motorcycling can be a lot of fun. You should achieve maximum safety, and that starts with personal abilities. Experience only means that you have done things often. There are good and bad experiences. Then there are people who have been riding a motorcycle for 40 years, but still have no experience in some areas. As previously indicated, if you are really interested in riding a motorcycle, then you should take drivers training at the Nordschleife.

A word to the speeders: The definition of speeding is to move at the highest possible speed. This is an "art." Of course, public roads are not the suitable place for it. The average driver has poor judgment for high speed, much less being able to deal with it.

Therefore, practice restraint and be considerate!

Wolfgang Fries

About the author

I, Wolfgang Fries, was born in St. Wendel/Saarland, Germany on January 16, 1966. I had a standard education that included technical school. Afterward, I served five years in the Bundeswehr (German army) until 1994, when I started working as a stucco master, an occupation that enriched my life. I was easily able to form social contacts and was still well-liked after work. By forming a few friendships, I felt a social bond with others.

Unfortunately, I had to stop this nice work. As it turned out, bad things can lead to a good result. If I were not sitting in a wheelchair, I never would have written all of this. During a disastrous accident with the motorcycle, I broke my spine and since then have been permanently paralyzed. It happened on a public road while riding straight. Braking before a curve, I lost control after hitting an oil slick.

But there is something in life everyone should know: Life itself. During all the work one does, and all the good times one enjoys, one should never forget this. Exactly that was my endeavor.

It is not easy to find out what or who you are. If you're a tradesman, engineer, thinker, or racing professional ...

You can be anything, you only have to decide!

Weitere Bücher

Philosophie des Lebens - Das Buch der Grundlagen -

Was sind die Grundlagen des Daseins? Welche Geisteshaltung bedarf es in der heutigen Zeit um im Leben bestehen zu können, um Glück und Wohlergehen zu erfahren? Was ist wichtig zu wissen?

Der Mensch selbst, als denkendes Wesen ist der Ansicht, dass seine mächtigste Waffe der Verstand ist. Aufgrund seiner Fähigkeit zu denken hat er sich die Erde zum Untertan gemacht. Und tatsächlich, das Denken bestimmt das Handeln des Menschen, der Mensch ist nur so stabil wie sein Gedanke.

Der Gedanke selbst fußt auf Grundlagen die bestimmend dazu sind, wie man überlebt. So versucht der Mensch sich selbst, sein Denken und Handeln, die Welt um sich herum zu verstehen.

Verstehen: Was ist wichtiger als Verstehen selbst?

Grundlagen komprimiert verpackt, in kurzen Texten dargestellt. Mehr als 200 Essays führen den Leser zu mehr Verstehen im Leben und über das Leben selbst, sei es nun über den Menschen, das Denken, Glücklichsein, Beziehung, Lernen, Beruf, den Ursprung von Krankheiten, gesellschaftliches Dasein, Religion, Politik oder Freiheit.

Die Probleme des Menschen werden von der Ursache her geschildert und Lösungen angeboten. Es macht einen Unterschied dieses Wissen zu haben und sich dadurch selbst zu helfen.

Als Taschenbuch oder als Bibliotheken-Ausgabe im extra stabilen Hardcover-Format und Fadenbindung herausgegeben. „Philosophie des Lebens – Das Buch der Grundlagen" ist der Gesamt-Band welcher die Bücher „Meine Philosophie", „Lernen wie man lernt, lernen wie man versteht", „Eine glückliche Beziehung führen", „Rückführung – Einführung und Kurzanleitung" und ehemals „Im Leben bestehen – Die Bibel des 21sten Jahrhunderts" in einem Buch vereint.

Philosophie des Lebens - Das Buch der Grundlagen -; 656 Seiten, 2017.

ISBN: **978-3-7357-8561-9** - Hardcover,

ISBN: **978-3-7460-2923-8** - Taschenbuch

Menschenrechte und Pflichten - revidiert

Die Gewährleistung der Menschrechte in einer geordneten Umgebung ist das Fundament für ein friedliches Zusammensein und einer gedeihenden Zivilisation. In einer feindlichen Umgebung mit Kämpfen und Zerstörung gibt es kein friedliches Zusammensein und keine gedeihende Zivilisation, welche durch ihre Errungenschaften in Medizin, Technik und den Wissenschaften zur Wohlfahrt des Menschen beiträgt.

Aber was zeichnet die Menschenrechte nun aus, dass diese zu einem friedlichen Zusammenleben führen und zum Wohlergehen des Menschen beitragen?

Zuerst braucht der Mensch die grundlegende Einstellung und dann entsprechendes Wissen und einen Kodex um dies zu verwirklichen. Es ist also eine Sache an der jeder einzelne arbeiten muss.

Menschenrechte und Pflichten - revidiert; 32 Seiten, 2017

ISBN: **978-3-7460-1913-0**